English Skills 4

Answers

Carol Matchett

Schofield & Sims

Which book?

The **English Skills** books are aligned with the end-of-year objectives for Key Stage 2. For the majority of pupils aged seven to 11 years, follow the guidance given on page 2 as to which book to use with each year group.

If a pupil is working significantly above or below the standard normally expected for his or her age, another book may be more appropriate. If you are not sure which to choose, **Workbook descriptors** and a simple **Entry test** are available to help you identify the book that is best suited to the pupil's abilities. You can also use these resources with new pupils joining your class or school.

Photocopy masters of the **Workbook descriptors** and **Entry test** are provided in the **Teacher's Guide** – which also contains the **Entry test marking key**, full instructions for use, and a range of other **English Skills** copymasters. For ordering details, see page 46.

You may be using **English Skills** at Key Stage 3 or with other mixed-ability groups of young people or adults. In such cases you will find the **Workbook descriptors** and **Entry test** vital in deciding which book to give each student.

Published by Schofield & Sims Ltd,
Dogley Mill, Fenay Bridge, Huddersfield HD8 0NQ, UK
Telephone 01484 607080

www.schofieldandsims.co.uk

Copyright © Schofield and Sims Ltd, 2011
Fourth impression 2015

Author: Carol Matchett
Carol Matchett has asserted her moral right under the Copyright, Designs and Patents Act, 1988, to be identified as the author of this work.

British Library Cataloguing in Publication Data
A catalogue record for this book is available from the British Library.

All rights reserved. Except where otherwise indicated, no part of this publication may be reproduced, stored in a retrieval system, or transmitted in any form or by any means, electronic, mechanical, photocopying, recording or otherwise, without either the prior permission of the publisher or a licence permitting restricted copying in the United Kingdom issued by the Copyright Licensing Agency Limited, Saffron House, 6–10 Kirby Street, London EC1N 8TS.

The **Writing task assessment sheets** (pages 16, 30 and 44) and the **Completed proofreading tasks** (pages 17, 31 and 45) are exempt from these restrictions and may be photocopied for use within the purchaser's institution only.

Commissioning and editorial project management by
Carolyn Richardson Publishing Services (www.publiserve.co.uk)

Design by **Ledgard Jepson Ltd**
Printed in the UK by **Wyndeham Grange Ltd**, Southwick, West Sussex

Book 4 Answers ISBN 978 07217 1184 3

Contents

Schofield & Sims English Skills 4 Answers

Teacher's notes 2

SECTION 1

Answers to Tests 1 to 12, covering: 4

Spelling: Common letter strings with different pronunciations. Common homophones. Spelling rules and patterns: plurals (words ending with **f**); **ible**, **able**; high-frequency words with unstressed vowels.

Word structure: Adding **ive**, **ist**, **able**. Compound words. Hyphens. Exploring common roots.

Vocabulary: Using word structures and common roots to work out meaning. Synonyms and shades of meaning. Adverbs. Idioms.

Sentence structure: Exploring sentence types and alternative sentence constructions; adding phrases and clauses; using a range of connectives.

Punctuation: Commas to mark clauses and phrases; avoiding comma splice. Setting out and punctuating dialogue. Apostrophes for possession (including plurals). Identifying more advanced punctuation (dash, colon).

Grammar: Choosing words for impact and effect; figurative and expressive language. Language features of different text types. Verb tenses; using auxiliary verbs. Formal and informal language. Direct and reported speech.

Section 1 Writing task assessment sheet: Jam sandwich! 16

Section 1 Completed proofreading task: Ricky the runner 17

SECTION 2

Answers to Tests 1 to 12, covering all the above, plus: 18

Spelling: Different spellings of 'shun' endings. Regular spelling patterns (soft **g**, soft **c**) and rules relating to double consonants.

Word structure: Less common prefixes. Word families.

Vocabulary: Formal and informal synonyms. Words with multiple antonyms or with several meanings. Using prefixes to create antonyms. Onomatopoeia. Everyday metaphors.

Sentence structure: Question types. Combining sentences; pronouns as connectives. Adapting sentence structures to different story text types.

Punctuation: Punctuation in longer sentences. Using brackets and dashes.

Grammar: Similes; metaphors. Standard English. Noun types. Possessive pronouns.

Section 2 Writing task assessment sheet: The tortoise and the hare 30

Section 2 Completed proofreading task: Fruity fruit salad 31

SECTION 3

Answers to Tests 1 to 12, covering all the above, plus: 32

Spelling: Spelling unstressed vowels in polysyllabic words. Regular spelling patterns (**ie**, **ei**). Adding vowel suffixes. **i** before **e**.

Word structure: Less common prefixes (**pro**, **sus**, **ir**) and suffixes (**ify**, **ise**, **ism**, **ity**).

Vocabulary: Words with an everyday and a subject-specific meaning; technical words. Word formation; compound words.

Sentence structure: Adapting sentence construction to different text types, purposes or readers. Prepositional phrases. Combining clauses.

Punctuation: Use and misuse of apostrophes and commas. Punctuation to clarify meaning; commas to embed.

Grammar: Words for specific aims. Text types. Prepositions. Modal verbs.

Section 3 Writing task assessment sheet: Outraged 44

Section 3 Completed proofreading task: The genie of the bedside lamp 45

Full list of the Schofield & Sims English Skills books 46

Teacher's notes

Introduction to the series

Schofield & Sims English Skills provides regular and carefully graded practice in key literacy skills. It is designed for use alongside your existing literacy lessons, embedding key aspects of grammar, sentence structure, punctuation and spelling and constantly revisiting them until they become automatic. At the same time it reinforces and develops pupils' knowledge of word structure and vocabulary.

Each workbook comprises three sections with 12 tests in each one. The tests become more difficult, but the increase in difficulty is gradual. The workbooks are fully compatible with the Key Stage 2 literacy curriculum and the final tests in each book are aligned with the end-of-year objectives as follows:

- **Book 1:** Year 2
- **Book 3:** Year 4
- **Book 5:** Year 6
- **Book 2:** Year 3
- **Book 4:** Year 5
- **Book 6:** Years 6/7

Please note: Pupils working towards the objectives for an earlier year should use the appropriate workbook. There is no need for all members of the class to be working on the same book at the same time.

Parts A, B and C

Each test is divided into three parts:

- Part A: **Warm-up** – puzzles, 'warm-up' exercises and revision of earlier learning
- Part B: **Word work** – spelling, word structure, exploring words and their meanings
- Part C: **Sentence work** – putting words together to make sentences: for example, choosing suitable words, forming and punctuating sentences or checking for grammatical accuracy.

Answering the test questions

After you have demonstrated to the class how some of the different question types are to be answered, the pupils work through the test items without adult help – either individually or in pairs. For Books 2 to 6, encourage them to refer to dictionaries, thesauruses and other reference materials rather than asking for your help. The tests may be used flexibly. For example, a test may be tackled in one session or over several days.

Marking

This book provides correct answers for **English Skills 4**; where various different answers would be acceptable, an example is provided. The **Focus** panel stating the areas of learning being tested helps you to decide whether the pupil's answer is satisfactory. **Please note and explain to the class that if all or part of a question has several possible answers, the question number is displayed like this 5 . If a question has a specific answer, the question number is displayed like this 5 . It is displayed in this way even if the answer is made up of several parts that may be given in any order.**

Some questions test more than one area: for example, a question on writing in the past tense might also check pupils' knowledge of the spelling rules for adding **ed**. In such cases, both parts of the answer must be correct, reflecting real-life situations that require varied knowledge and skills.

Group marking sessions

Group or class marking sessions led by the teacher or classroom assistant are the most effective way of marking the tests: pupils learn by comparing and discussing answers.

Another benefit of group or class marking sessions is that they highlight deficits in pupils' knowledge, which will inform your future teaching. Where pupils have given a wrong answer, or none at all, briefly reinforce the key teaching point using an item from this book as a model. In a plenary discussion at the end of the session, encourage pupils to evaluate their own successes; each pupil can then work with a 'talk partner' to record areas needing improvement and discuss appropriate learning objectives.

Suggested questions to ask in a marking session:
- How many different 'correct' answers did we come up with?
- Were some sentence or word choices more interesting or effective than others? Why?
- How do you know this answer is correct?
- How can we make the answer correct?
- Is there an answer that would be even better?
- What are the success criteria for this type of question?
- What are the key points to remember next time?
- When might we put these key points into practice in our reading or writing?

Marking the end-of-section assessments

At the end of each workbook section are two writing assessments: the independent writing task and the proofreading task. These check that pupils are applying in their writing the knowledge, skills and understanding developed in the weekly tests. The assessments also provide evidence of a pupil's strengths and weaknesses, which will help you to set appropriate targets. You might consider sharing with the pupils a simplified version of the mark scheme – and then involve them in setting their own targets, as discussed above.

- *The independent writing task*

The independent writing task gives you a snapshot of a pupil's writing development. Prompts help pupils to plan and gather ideas so that when they begin writing they can focus on expressing their ideas clearly and effectively. On pages 16, 30 and 44 you will find photocopiable **Writing task assessment sheets** – one for each section – with specific assessment points arranged under the headings 'Sentence structure and punctuation', 'Composition and effect' and 'Spelling'. Complete one of these sheets as you mark each pupil's work.

- *The proofreading task*

The proofreading task focuses on punctuation, grammar and spelling. Examples of **Completed proofreading tasks** for each section, also photocopiable, are supplied on pages 17, 31 and 45. However, please note that pupils may choose to correct some of the errors using methods different to those shown in the example but equally valid. For example, two unpunctuated strings of words might be joined using a connective or separated to make two sentences. Additional evidence gained from the relevant proofreading task will help you to further assess pupils' achievements in 'Sentence punctuation' and 'Spelling' as already assessed in the writing task. If you wish, you can use the photocopiable sheet to make notes on a pupil's work.

Please note: Pupils whose scores against the assessment statements are low do not need to repeat a section. All the books revisit difficult areas and offer ample opportunities for further practice. Instead of holding a pupil back, highlight the assessment statements that reveal his or her weaknesses and use these to set learning targets. Ensure that pupils know their targets as they begin the next section.

Progress chart

On page 46 of the pupil workbook only you will find a **Progress chart**, with one column each for Sections 1, 2 and 3, and a list of 'I can' statements relating to the kinds of activities practised in the section. Please ask every pupil to complete the relevant column when they have finished working through a section.

The **Progress chart** encourages pupils to monitor their own work by identifying those activities that they have mastered and those requiring further attention. When pupils colour in the chart as recommended (**green** for **easy**, **orange** for **getting there** and **red** for **difficult**) it gives a clear picture of progress. It also shows the benefits of systematic practice: an activity that the pupil cannot perform in Section 1 later gets the 'green light'.

The **Progress chart** promotes assessment for learning and personalised learning. Whilst it is best completed in the workbook, so that achievements in all sections may be compared, you may at some point wish to have additional copies. For this reason, it may be photocopied. **However, all other pages of the pupil workbook remain strictly non-photocopiable.**

Section 1   Test 1

A   WARM-UP

Add an adverb.

1. She spoke _hesitantly_ about her feelings.
2. He was _severely_ punished for the crime.
3. _Casually_, they walked off down the road.

Add one or two consonants to complete the words.

4. wor**d**   wor**k**   wor**m**
5. wor**l**d   wor**t**h   wor**st**

Put the letters in order to make a word.

6. e g s s u — _guess_
7. a c h t w — _watch_
8. e h l o w — _whole_

PART A Focus
1–3: using and positioning of adverbs
4–8: visual spelling strategies
9–10: prefixes

Add the same prefix to each set of words.

9. _al_ most   _al_ though   _al_ mighty
10. _ex_ change   _ex_ claim   _ex_ tend

B   WORD WORK

Write the root word. Underline the prefixes and suffix/es.

1. d i s a p p r o v i n g l y — _approve_
2. i m p e r s o n a l — _person_

Change the noun in **bold** into a plural.

3. one **thief** → three _thieves_
4. one **Princess** → three _Princesses_
5. Penny's **puppy** → _Penny's puppies_
6. the brave **child** → _the brave children_

PART B Focus
1–2: word structure
3–6: spelling patterns; pluralisation
7–10: synonyms; shades of meaning

Sort the words into two groups.

frustrated   livid   irritated   enraged

7. **very angry:** _livid, enraged_
8. **quite angry:** _frustrated, irritated_

Add two synonyms to each group.

9. **very happy:** _ecstatic, overjoyed_
10. **quite happy:** _pleased, content_

C   SENTENCE WORK

Complete the sentence.

1. After _everyone had calmed down_, we had a great time.
2. Despite _the terrible weather_, we had a great time.
3. Although _the campsite was disappointing_, we had a great time.
4. Before _the rains came_, we had a great time.

PART C Focus
1–4: using connectives linking clauses
5–8: sentence modification: using adverbs and adjectives
9–10: misuse of commas

Improve the sentence by adding three suitable words.

5. The _handsome_ _young_ man walked along the road, singing _happily_ to himself.
6. Ellie gazed _wistfully_ out of the window at the _crowded_ city _below_.
7. The _little_ dog looked at him with his _sad_ _brown_ eyes.
8. The women looked _sadly_ around the _bare_ _empty_ room.

It was beginning to rain, big heavy drops fell from the sky, the picnic was over

9. What is wrong with the punctuation? _Commas are used where stronger punctuation is needed._
10. Write it correctly.

   It was beginning to rain. Big heavy drops fell from the sky. The picnic was over.

4   X DEFINITIVE ANSWER   X SAMPLE ANSWER

Section 1   Test 2

A   WARM-UP

Complete the simile using a suitable animal.

1. mad as *a monkey*
2. cheerful as *a laughing hyena*
3. lazy as *a sleepy sloth*
4. greedy as *a guzzling goat*

Add the missing suffix to complete the word.

5. w i l l **ing** n e s s
6. w o r t h **less** n e s s
7. f o o l **ish** n e s s

PART A Focus
1–4: word play; similes
5–7: word structure
8–10: visual spelling strategies

Write a word using these letters. The letters must be used in this order.

8. t g t — *target*
9. p s b — *possible*
10. c m n — *common*

B   WORD WORK

One consonant or two? Write in the missing letters.

1. s h a **d** o w (d)
2. s h a **ll** o w (l)

PART B Focus
1–4: double and single consonant spellings
5–7: spelling of homophones
8–10: meaning of common roots

Underline the correct word of the two that appear in brackets.

3. The water (sloped / <u>slopped</u>) around.
4. How did you know? *Because water 'slops' and the past tense is 'slopped'.*
5. Edgar (<u>stares</u> / stairs) out of the window.
6. How did you know? *Because 'stares' means looks and 'stairs' means steps.*
7. Write the homophone.
   morning *mourning*   seen *scene*

All three words come from the same root. Underline the root.

8. <u>therm</u>al <u>therm</u>ometer <u>therm</u>ostat
9. <u>aqua</u>rium <u>aque</u>duct <u>Aqua</u>rius

What do the root words mean?

10. therm = *heat*   aqua = *water*

C   SENTENCE WORK

Turn each sentence into a question (Q) and an imperative (I).

1. Let's go to the cinema.
   Q: *Shall we go to the cinema?*
   I: *Go to the cinema.*
2. You could bake a cake.
   Q: *Would you like to bake a cake?*
   I: *Bake a cake.*
3. We could form two teams.
   Q: *Shall we form two teams?*
   I: *Form two teams.*

Add words to create the given mood.

4. **calm, peaceful**   The *soft* moonlight gave a *delicate* glow to the *whispering* trees.
5. **threatening, sinister**   The *pale* moonlight gave a *n eerie* glow to the *shadowy* trees.
6. Underline the word that best describes your additions.   verbs <u>adjectives</u> nouns adverbs

PART C Focus
1–3: questions and imperatives
4–6: adjectives for mood
7–10: apostrophes for possession

Rewrite the phrase using three words only.

7. the instruments belonging to the band — *the band's instruments*
8. the party held for the three brothers — *the brothers' party*
9. the club belonging to the supporters — *the supporters' club*
10. the staffroom for the teachers — *the teachers' staffroom*

X DEFINITIVE ANSWER   X SAMPLE ANSWER

Section 1   Test 3

A   WARM-UP

lion   sandwich

1. Write a sentence using these words.
   A lion stole my sandwich.

2. Write a question using these words.
   Did a lion really steal your sandwich?

Add the missing vowels.
You may use a letter twice if necessary.

a e u

3. b_e_a_u_t y
4. _a_u_t_u_m n
5. b_e_c_a_u_s e
6. p_a_u_se

7. These words and prefixes are mixed up.
   Write them correctly.
   minisecond   microbus   nanochip
   minibus, microchip, nanosecond

8. What do the word roots have in common?
   They are all to do with smallness.

Write two more words with the root shown in **bold**.

9. **mini**   *minimum, miniature*
10. **micro**   *microphone, microscope*

PART A Focus
1–2: forming sentences and questions
3–6: spelling patterns
7–10: meaning of common roots

B   WORD WORK

Write in the missing word.

I can do it myself.

1. She can do it _herself_.
2. We can do it _ourselves_.
3. They can do it _themselves_.

Make three words.

press im de ing ly ure

4. _impress_
5. _depressingly_
6. _pressure_

Write the meaning of the phrase.

7. to turn over a new leaf
   to make a fresh start

8. to feel under the weather
   to feel unwell

9. That rings a bell!
   That sounds familiar!

10. What do you notice about these phrases?
    They are idioms and are not meant to be taken literally.

PART B Focus
1–3: reflexive pronouns; plural spellings
4–6: word structure; prefixes and suffixes
7–10: idiomatic phrases

C   SENTENCE WORK

Continue the sentence, to explain or tell the reader more.

1. People are uneasy *about what might happen in the future.*
2. Josh ran through the door *, waving the letter in excitement.*
3. Fold the paper in half *so that you make a triangle shape.*
4. The dog watched the cat *with interest from behind the tree.*

Mobile phones should be switched off.

Rewrite the sentence as

5. a question: *Have you switched off your mobile phone?*
6. an imperative: *Switch off your mobile phone.*
7. an exclamation: *Switch off now!*

Write the dialogue correctly.

8. We must leave said David.   *"We must leave," said David.*
9. When asked Anna.   *"When?" asked Anna.*
10. Very soon David replied.   *"Very soon," David replied.*

PART C Focus
1–4: extending sentences; adding phrases and clauses to clarify
5–7: questions, imperatives, exclamations
8–10: punctuating direct speech

6   X DEFINITIVE ANSWER   X SAMPLE ANSWER

Section 1 Test 4

A WARM-UP

Add the correct word endings.

1. The rain fell heavy__ily__, make__ing__ the fields mist__y__ and grey.
2. Luck__ily__, the drive__r__ stop__ped__ the car before hit__ting__ the two parked lorr__ies__.

Complete the word sum.

3. occupy + ing = __occupying__
4. occupy + ed = __occupied__
5. occupy + er = __occupier__

PART A Focus
1–5: rules for adding word endings
6: homophones
7–10: word play; alliteration

6. Write the homophone.
   threw __through__   heard __herd__

Complete the alliterative pattern.

ten tigers tickling to tease

7. nine newts __needing to know__
8. seven swans __starting to swim__
9. five frogs __failing to feed__
10. two turtles __trying to talk__

B WORD WORK

The same letter string is missing from all these words. Write it in.

1. e n __ough__   a l t h __ough__
2. t h r __ough__   t h __ough__ t
3. What do you notice? __The letter string can make different sounds.__
4. Write two more words with this letter string.
   __cough, bough__

Draw a line to join the word to another word with the same root.

5. noun — vocal
6. voice — announce
7. annual — anniversary

PART B Focus
1–4: common letter strings with different sounds
5–9: word roots
10: adverbs with similar meanings

Write two words that use the root word.

8. graph __graphic, autograph__
9. circum __circumference, circumstance__

10. Underline the synonyms of **sadly**.
    politely __dejectedly__ gleefully __dismally__

C SENTENCE WORK

Complete the simile.

1. A still pond is like __a mirror to the sky.__
2. Autumn leaves are like __burnished butterflies.__
3. A volcano is like __a dragon that breathes fire.__
4. A poppy is like __red tissue paper.__

Cross out some of the words and write new ones that make the performance sound more impressive.

5. Cleaver ~~sent a~~ ~~good~~ high ball into the penalty area and Jones ~~got it into the net~~.
   __lofted, terrific, rose to head it home__
6. The goalkeeper ~~jumped well~~ and ~~knocked~~ the ball just over the crossbar.
   __dived full length, tipped__
7. After some ~~good~~ play from Cleaver, Robinson ~~sent a good~~ ball past the stranded keeper.
   __brilliant, curved a masterful__

Add the missing commas.

8. Although it was dark, I knew someone was following me.
9. Before we begin, let's check everyone is here.
10. The two children, who were very tired, soon fell fast asleep.

PART C Focus
1–4: using figurative language; similes
5–7: language used for emphasis or effect
8–10: using commas to mark clauses

X DEFINITIVE ANSWER   X SAMPLE ANSWER

Section 1 Test 5

A WARM-UP

Complete the sentence.

1. Sam made tea. Meanwhile, **Jon sat by the fire and read the paper.**
2. Sam made tea. Suddenly, **a crashing sound came from the living room.**
3. Sam made tea. Afterwards, **they all sat at the table to eat it.**

Add the same three-letter word to all three words.

4. **ear**th   s**ear**ch   h**ear**d
5. cr**eat**ure   gr**eat**est   sw**eat**
6. flav**our**   col**our**   j**our**ney

7. Underline the word that is **not** a real word.

   artist novelist <u>photographist</u> stockist

Write three more words ending with **ist**.

8. scientist
9. dentist
10. balloonist

PART A Focus
1–3: connectives to link ideas or events
4–6: spelling strategies; letter strings
7–10: the suffix ist

B WORD WORK

Add **ible** or **able**.

1. suit **able**   enjoy **able**   fashion **able**
2. terr **ible**   ed **ible**   horr **ible**
3. How are the **able** words different from the **ible** words?
   'able' is added when there is already a whole word there.

Add a word after the hyphen to complete the compound word.

4. break-**in**   *Clue:* burglary
5. passer-**by**   *Clue:* someone walking past
6. Add a prefix before the hyphen.
   co-operate   **non**-stick   **ex**-president
7. Write three more examples of words with hyphens.
   anti-clockwise, non-fiction, co-star

Write a definition.

8. **disapprovingly:** as if you don't approve
9. **enthusiastically:** excitedly
10. **courteously:** politely

PART B Focus
1–3: the spelling patterns able and ible
4–7: words joined with hyphens
8–10: the meaning of adverbs; word structure

C SENTENCE WORK

Rewrite the sentence with the word or phrase in **bold** at the beginning.

1. The tent collapsed **as I stood up**.   As I stood up, the tent collapsed.
2. The room was **strangely** silent.   Strangely, the room was silent.
3. There was a faint rumble **from far away**.   From far away, there was a faint rumble.

Write **formal** or **informal** beside each sentence to identify the type of language used.

4. I was travelling along Northgate Road when the accident occurred.   formal
5. There I was minding my own business and guess what happened?   informal

Give one reason for each of your answers.

6. 4 uses formal words (e.g., 'occurred').
7. 5 sounds more like a conversation.

What punctuation mark is hidden by the symbol?

8. He might have won a thousand pounds ▲ or even a million ♠
   ▲ is **a dash**   ♠ is **an exclamation mark**
9. For this experiment you will need the following▼ a bottle● filter paper and a paper clip.
   ▼ is **a colon**   ● is **a comma**
10. Sally♦sadly♦▼ Are you sure■   *Clue:* this is a line of dialogue from a playscript
    ♦ is **a bracket**   ▼ is **a colon**   ■ is **a question mark**

PART C Focus
1–3: reordering sentences
4–7: formal and informal language
8–10: more complex punctuation

Section 1 Test 6

A WARM-UP

Write three sentences using these words only.

waited they nervously

1 They waited nervously.
2 Nervously, they waited.
3 They nervously waited.

4 Add the **ing** ending.

spiral ling   crackle ing   explode ing

Draw a line to join the word to a suffix and make a new word.

5 free ——— ship
6 false ——— hood
7 partner ——— dom

Write the noun as a plural.

8 **battery** batteries
9 **box** boxes
10 **knife** knives

PART A Focus
1–3: word order; moving adverbs
4: rules for adding verb endings
5–7: suffixes
8–10: plural spelling rules

B WORD WORK

Add the missing vowels.

1 g a r d e n
2 g o l d e n
3 h e a v e n
4 d i f f e r e n t

PART B Focus
1–4: unstressed vowels; high-frequency words
5–6: adding **tion**
7–10: formal synonyms for frequently-used words

5 Add the suffix **tion**.

inform ation   tempt ation   expect ation

6 What do you notice?

An 'a' is added to make the word easier to say.

7 Underline the two synonyms that sound the most formal.

lots <u>ample</u> heaps loads bags <u>sufficient</u>

Write two more formal synonyms.

8 **get** obtain, acquire
9 **give** provide, donate
10 **tell** inform, notify

C SENTENCE WORK

1 Write eight verbs that would be suitable to fill the gap.

Mr Jackson _____ come home.

has, might, could, will, may, had, should, must

2 Write two words that would form the past tense. had, did
3 Write two words that would form the future tense. might, will

Write two adverbs that give different views of the character.

4 "What are you doing?" asked the boy politely / sharply .
5 "Come on then," said Maria cheerfully / gloomily .
6 "I'll take that," the woman said greedily / helpfully .

PART C Focus
1–3: modal verbs; tenses
4–6: adverbs
7–10: using colons, dashes, commas, brackets in sentences

Continue the sentence.

7 The year is divided into four seasons: spring, summer, autumn and winter.
8 Jack finally arrived – only an hour late!
9 Before he knew it, the train had left without him.
10 We had pizza for tea (my favourite).

Section 1   Test 7

A   WARM-UP

Write the imperative as a question.

1. Stand up.
   Can you stand up?

2. Come here.
   Could you come here?

3. Go and play.
   Why don't you go and play?

Add the same prefix to all three words.

4. _de_ code   _de_ form   _de_ flate
5. _re_ place   _re_ move   _re_ view
6. _mis_ take _mis_ count _mis_ lead

Write in the missing word.

it's   its

7. _It's_ great here!
8. The dog buried _its_ bone.
9. The tree shook _its_ leaves.
10. I hope _it's_ not too late.

PART A Focus
1–3: imperatives; questions
4–6: prefixes
7–10: using it's and its

B   WORD WORK

Change the nouns into plurals.

1. piano _s_   radio _s_
2. potato _es_   hero _es_
3. What is the same about the spelling of the singular words?
   They all end with 'o'.
4. How are the plurals different?
   In 1 you add 's' to make a plural;
   in 2 you add 'es'.

These words are mixed up. Write them correctly.

sublight atmomerge micronatural supersphere

5. _submerge_   7. _atmosphere_
6. _microlight_   8. _supernatural_

Write three words that use the root word.

9. **verb** (meaning **word**):
   verbose, verbal, adverb

10. **uni** (meaning **one**):
    unit, uniform, unity

PART B Focus
1–4: plurals of words ending with vowels
5–10: word roots

C   SENTENCE WORK

Write three sentences that contain these words.

thieves   boxes

1. a simple sentence: _The thieves stole several boxes of clothing._
2. a compound sentence: _Thieves broke into a warehouse but took only empty boxes._
3. a sentence with a connective: _As the thieves fled, they dropped the boxes._

PART C Focus
1–3: sentence construction
4–7: possessive apostrophes
8–9: language for effect
10: story genre

Complete the phrase and add apostrophes to show which of these groups owns what.

the driver   the bakers   the crew   the horses

4. _the bakers'_ oven
5. _the driver's_ van
6. _the horses'_ stables
7. _the crew's_ spaceship

Complete the sentence, choosing words for effect.

8. The man _plunged_ into the woods, branches _cracking_ under his feet, the beast _clawing_ at his coat.
9. He saw its _fearsome_ eyes, round like _saucers_. He smelt its _filthy_ coat of _matted_ fur.
10. What type of story are both these sentences from? Underline your chosen answer.

   science fiction   <u>horror story</u>   school story

Section 1   Test 8

A   WARM-UP

Add an adverb to make the statement stronger.

1 This is __clearly__ wrong.

2 __Surely__, no-one can agree with this!

One consonant or two? Write in the missing letters.

3 m o _m_ e n t (m)

4 c o _ff_ e e (f)

5 t a _tt_ o o (t)

PART A Focus
1–2: adverbs to clarify point of view
3–5: single and double consonants
6–7: words ending with vowels
8–10: similes

Add the missing vowels.   **Clue: all foods**

6 b _a_ n _a_ n _a_   s _a_ m _o_ s _a_

7 r a v _i_ o l _i_   r _i_ s _o_ tt _o_

The flob is an imaginary creature.
Complete these similes to describe it.

8 It moves like __a caterpillar.__

9 It sounds like __a squelching jelly.__

10 It eats like __a vacuum cleaner.__

B   WORD WORK

Add the missing letters.

1 p o s s _i_ b l e   3 r e m a r k _a_ b l e

2 v i s _i_ b l e   4 r e a s o n _a_ b l e

Add a prefix and/or a suffix to make a new word.

5 __mis__ take __n__   **Clue: wrong**

6 __im__ prison __ed__ **Clue: locked up**

7 active __ity__   **Clue: a task to do**

Complete the well-known saying and write a definition.

8 you can't judge a book by __its cover__
   means: __don't make judgements based on appearances__

9 got out of bed on __the wrong side__
   means: __in a bad mood__

10 over the __moon__
   means: __very pleased__

PART B Focus
1–4: ible and able
5–7: word structure
8–10: idioms

C   SENTENCE WORK

Write a sentence to follow the headline.

1 Class G takes the plunge!   __On Friday, Class G at Welford Primary school braved the chilly weather with a sponsored swim.__

2 School concert raises the roof!   __A concert on Tuesday by pupils at Welford Primary school received enthusiastic applause.__

3 Bookbusters are go!   __The first meeting of a new after-school book club was held this Monday.__

Write the tense used for each line of this script.

4 **Ben and Angie enter, running.**   present tense

5 **Ben: No-one saw us.**   past tense

6 **Angie: What shall we do if someone comes?**   future tense

PART C Focus
1–3: introductory sentences
4–6: tenses
7–10: punctuating direct speech

Rewrite the sentence as direct speech.

7 Eve asked Ross if he was OK.   "Are you OK, Ross?" asked Eve.

8 Mr Bahra said his house was ruined.   "My house is ruined," said Mr Bahra.

9 The genie told him the magic word [yoyo].   "The magic word is 'yoyo'," said the genie.

10 Lucy asked for her size [size 2].   "Do you have a size 2?" asked Lucy.

X DEFINITIVE ANSWER   **X SAMPLE ANSWER**

11

Section 1   Test 9

A   WARM-UP

Continue the sentence.

1. Terry was anxious in case _someone had seen him._
2. Terry was anxious despite _the fact that he was well prepared._
3. Terry was anxious whenever _he was left alone in the house._
4. Terry was anxious until _Sam arrived._

PART A Focus
1–4: using conjunctions
5–7: word roots
8–10: spelling rules and patterns

Write two words with this root.

5. **tri** (means 3)   _triangle, triathlon_
6. **octo** (means 8)   _octagon, octopus_
7. **dec** (means 10)   _decimal, decade_

Cross out the word that is wrongly spelt. Write the correct spelling.

8. special social ~~parcial~~   _partial_
9. yoyos ~~echos~~ solos   _echoes_
10. reliable ~~edable~~ adorable   _edible_

B   WORD WORK

Add the missing syllable.

1. f r i g h t _en_ i n g
2. f o r _mal_ l y
3. i n _ter_ e s t
4. g e n _er_ a l

PART B Focus
1–4: syllables; unstressed vowels
5–6: rules for adding **tion**
7–10: root words; word structure

5. Write the new word that is made by adding the suffix **tion**.

   protect   _protection_
   invent   _invention_
   perfect   _perfection_
   illustrate _illustration_

6. What do you notice?
   The words drop the 't' or 'te' ending when you add 'tion'.

Write three words using the root word.

7. child   _children, childhood, childlike_
8. pain   _painful, painless, painstaking_
9. hand   _handle, handler, handkerchief_
10. move   _moveable, movie, remove_

C   SENTENCE WORK

What type of instructional text is each instruction taken from?

PART C Focus
1–6: the features of instructions
7–10: reordering sentences

1. **Bake until the top is golden and the fruit soft.**   from _a recipe_
2. **Select the text you want to change.**   from _a computer manual_
3. **Cut carefully along the dotted lines.**   from _instructions for making something_

Complete the sentence about instructions.

4. In instructions, verbs are usually _near the start of the sentence._
5. Adverbs are used to _say precisely how to do something._
6. Adjectives are used to _make the instructions clear and precise._

Rewrite the sentence so that the words and/or phrases are in a different order.

7. The door opened easily much to his surprise.   _Much to his surprise, the door opened easily._
8. Jack ran out of the door, grabbing the golden egg.
   Grabbing the golden egg, Jack ran out of the door.
9. Faintly, a light shone from far away.   _A light shone faintly from far away._
10. Amy forgot her worries for a while huddled by the fire.
    Huddled by the fire, Amy forgot her worries for a while.

Section 1   Test 10

A   WARM-UP
Complete the sentence.
1. Gradually, _the mist lifted._
2. Surprisingly, _the room was empty._
3. Determinedly, _he began to climb._

4. Write in the colours needed to complete these sayings.
   to see __red__   to feel __blue__
   a __grey__ area   a __golden__ opportunity

5. Write six compound words using the word **work**.
   workbench, workday, workhouse,
   workhorse, homework, workroom.

Add the missing vowels.
Clue: all musical instruments
6. b _a_ n j _o_
7. c _e_ ll _o_
8. p _i_ cc _o_ l _o_
9. b _o_ ng _o_
10. p _i_ _a_ n _o_

PART A Focus
1–3: using adverbs
4: idioms
5: compound words
6–10: words ending with vowels

B   WORD WORK
Add the missing letters.
1. s e v _e_ r a l   2. b u s _i_ n e s s

Cross out the words that are wrongly spelt. Write the correct spelling.

PART B Focus
1–2: unstressed vowels
3–5: checking for spelling errors
6–10: word roots; meanings

3. I had ~~sereal~~ for ~~brekfast~~.
   cereal, breakfast
4. I don't like ~~marmelade~~.   _marmalade_
5. Lunch was ~~too chickin samwichis~~ and an ~~appul~~.
   two chicken sandwiches, apple

6. Write four words using these roots only.
   auto para graph chute photo
   autograph, paragraph,
   photograph, parachute

Use the same roots to make two words that do **not** exist.
7. _autochute_   8. _paraphoto_

Write the meaning of the root word.
9. auto = _self_   10. photo = _light_

C   SENTENCE WORK
Write three different sentences using the word **shape**.
1. an instruction: _Draw round the shape and cut it out._
2. a headline: _Plans for new gym take shape_
3. a descriptive sentence: _In the darkness a shadowy shape moved across the lawn._

Write these formal statements so that they sound informal.
4. I am completely blameless. _I didn't do it._
5. Unfortunately, I am not able to provide that information. _Sorry, I can't help you._

Write this informal sentence so that it sounds formal.
6. People shouldn't do things like that. _Such behaviour is totally unacceptable._

Use brackets to add an extra comment or piece of information.
7. Auntie Agnes is coming on Saturday (_worst luck_).
8. My name is Richard (_Ricky to my friends_).
9. **Pirate 1** (_shouting_): Man overboard!
10. Raj (_who is my cousin_) came to tea.

PART C Focus
1–3: sentence types
4–6: formal and informal language
7–10: using brackets

X DEFINITIVE ANSWER   X SAMPLE ANSWER

Section 1   Test 11

A WARM-UP

Use the word **kitten** in each of the following.

1 **a sentence:** The kitten played with the ball.

2 **a headline:** Dramatic kitten rescue

3 **a question:** Have you seen my kitten?

4 **an order:** Leave the kitten alone.

Write three verbs to use in place of

5 **likes:** loves, adores, appreciates

6 **dislikes:** hates, loathes, despises

Add the missing vowels.

Clue: all animals

7 p u m a

8 a r m a d i l l o

9 d i n g o

10 k o a l a

PART A Focus
1–4: sentence types
5–6: synonyms
7–10: words ending with vowels

B WORD WORK

Underline the correct spelling.

1 slipery <u>slippery</u> slipperey slipprey

2 normaly normaley <u>normally</u> normerly

Add the suffix **able**.

3 **rely** reliable   **envy** enviable

4 **value** valuable   **adore** adorable

What two spelling rules did you use?

5 Change the 'y' to an 'i' to add 'able'.

6 Drop the final 'e' to add 'able'.

PART B Focus
1–2: rules for adding suffixes
3–6: rules for adding **able**
7–10: word roots

Auto means **self** or **one's own**.
Use this information to define

7 **automatic:** works by itself

8 **autograph:** in your own writing

Trans means **across**.
Use this information to define

9 **transatlantic:** across the Atlantic

10 **transplant:** to take from one place and move across to somewhere else

C SENTENCE WORK

Is this a simile or a metaphor? Write your answer.

1 Clouds are like cotton wool.   simile

2 Cotton wool clouds float by.   metaphor

3 Clouds are cotton wool in the sky.   metaphor

4 Clouds are white and soft as cotton wool.   simile

PART C Focus
1–6: similes and metaphors
7–9: punctuating speech; direct and reported speech
10: sentence formation

Write a simile and a metaphor about snowflakes.

5 **simile:** Snowflakes fall like blossom.

6 **metaphor:** Snowflakes are winter blossom in the frozen sky.

7 Add the punctuation to the dialogue.

Zoe: Have you seen this film?

Jack: No, I haven't.

8 Write the dialogue as direct speech.

"Have you seen this film?" asked Zoe.
"No, I haven't," replied Jack.

9 Write the dialogue as reported speech.   Zoe asked Jack if he had seen the film, but he hadn't.

10 Write a sentence using the words **girl rabbit although**.

The girl thought she had seen the rabbit although she wasn't sure.

Section 1   Test 12

A   WARM-UP

Write a simile to describe

1. **grass:** like a rug flung over the garden
2. **a spider's web:** like spokes on a wheel
3. **lightning:** like a crack in the sky

4. Underline the word that you **cannot** add **able** to.

   drink   port   bend   <u>water</u>   work

Add a prefix and a suffix.

5. <u>re</u> place <u>ment</u>   **Clue:** substitute
6. <u>de</u> sign <u>er</u>   **Clue:** someone who designs
7. <u>de</u> part <u>ure</u>   **Clue:** leaving

Add a letter to the middle of the word to make another word. Write the new word.

8. though — through
9. crate — create
10. widow — window

PART A Focus
1–3: similes
4–7: word structure
8–10: visual spelling strategies

B   WORD WORK

Add the suffix **tion**.

1. **combine** — combination
2. **vary** — variation

What two spelling rules did you use?

3. Drop the final 'e' to add 'ation'.
4. Change 'y' to 'i' to add 'ation'.

Imagine that the word in **bold** really existed. What would it mean?

5. **bivision:** seeing things twice
6. **supership:** a very large ship

Write a definition of these compound words, found in a computer manual.

7. **desktop:** the workspace on a computer screen
8. **download:** to copy files onto a computer
9. **online:** connected to the internet
10. **shortcut:** an icon providing a direct link

PART B Focus
1–4: adding tion
5–6: meaning of common word roots
7–10: subject-specific word meanings

C   SENTENCE WORK

Rewrite these statements in Standard English.

1. It felt real exciting seeing in the paper the picture what I drew.
   It felt really exciting seeing in the paper the picture that I had drawn.
2. I seen her eating them cakes what you brought.
   I saw her eating those cakes that you brought.
3. They was there. I seen them with me own eyes.   They were there. I saw them with my own eyes.
4. I didn't say nothing to no-one.   I didn't say anything to anyone.
5. Write a metaphor to describe a sunset.   The sky has been washed with orange paint.

Put a tick if the punctuation is correct. Put a cross if it is not.

6. "Dont drink that" screamed Josie. "Its Jakes magic potion."   ✗
7. He stood still. He listened. Not a sound could be heard.   ✓
8. The room was empty, there was no carpet on the floor.   ✗

Write the incorrect items correctly.

9. "Don't drink that!" screamed Josie. "It's Jake's magic potion!"
10. The room was empty. There was no carpet on the floor.

PART C Focus
1–4: Standard English
5: writing metaphors
6–10: checking punctuation

Remind the pupil to complete Section 1 of the Progress chart on page 46 of the workbook.

Schofield & Sims English Skills 4

Section 1 Writing task assessment sheet: Jam sandwich!

Name		Class/Set	
Teacher's name		Date	

Sentence structure and punctuation

	Always/often	Sometimes	Never
Uses varied connectives (e.g., **while**, **after**, **although**)			
Extends some sentences to clarify meaning			
Varies sentence construction			
Uses Standard English in news report			
Uses direct and reported speech, punctuated correctly			
Chooses appropriate tense (mainly past)			
Demarcates sentences accurately			
Uses commas to mark grammatical boundaries			
Uses apostrophes correctly			
Shows understanding of other punctuation (e.g., dash)			

Composition and effect

Shows clear sense of purpose			
Uses clearly identifiable sections and paragraphs			
Selects ideas to inform and engage (e.g., vital facts, interesting background information, comments)			
Connectives signal shifts in time, place, focus			
Language chosen for effect (e.g., headlines)			
Uses nouns precisely (e.g., proper nouns, expanded noun phrases)			
Uses powerful verbs for impact and precision			
Uses formal tone and language for newspaper report			

Spelling

Phonically regular words correctly spelt			
Applies rules for double and single consonants			
Common letter strings correctly spelt (e.g., **ough**)			
Tricky medium-frequency words correct			
Uses rules for adding prefixes and suffixes			
Spells suffixes correctly (e.g., **tion**, **ible**, **able**)			
Applies rules for adding verb endings			
Applies rules for spelling plurals			
Chooses correct homophone to fit context			

From: *English Skills 4 Answers* by Carol Matchett (ISBN 978 07217 1184 3). Copyright © Schofield & Sims Ltd, 2011. Published by Schofield & Sims Ltd, Dogley Mill, Fenay Bridge, Huddersfield HD8 0NQ, UK (www.schofieldandsims.co.uk). **This page may be photocopied for use within your school or institution only.**

Schofield & Sims English Skills 4
Section 1 Completed proofreading task: Ricky the runner

Name	Class/Set
Teacher's name	Date

Let me tell you about my br~~u~~other Ricky. He's ~~ate~~ eight years old, has spikey hair like a spid~~d~~er plant and a crook~~i~~ed smile that some ~~peepel~~ people think is ~~q~~cute. ~~me~~ Me, I just find it an^noying.

Nor~~me~~ally you will find him l~~ie~~ying on his bed with the r~~a~~emote in one hand and a ~~samwidge~~ sandwich (us~~eu~~ually s~~o~~ausage) in the other. TV's the most import~~u~~ant thing in his life^ and the own~~le~~y way to get his atten~~shun~~tion is to swi^tch it o^ff.

Now, bel~~i~~eve it or not, he says he's tur^ned over a ~~k~~new leaf and want^s to be a sporting su~~p~~perstar – just like that! "I'm going to be in the Olympics," he says. "I~~ts~~, ~~quiet~~ quite poss~~a~~ible I^ll be a gold medal~~est~~list," he tells us. ~~the~~ The boy's mad!

~~Enyway~~ Anyway, now he's jo~~g~~gging r~~ow~~ound the ho~~w~~use making us all su^ffer. ~~if~~ If that weren^t bad en~~uff~~ough, we have to put up with all his horrib~~ul~~le sports kit eve~~r~~ywhere. ~~am~~ Am I being ~~unreesonabul~~ unreasonable?

Section 1 tasks summary

Section 2   Test 1

A WARM-UP

Write three sentences and a question using these words only.

ready finally was she

1. She was finally ready.
2. Finally, she was ready.
3. She was ready – finally.
4. Was she finally ready?

Write two words using these letters. The letters must be used in this order.

5. m p t — complete, important
6. j m t — enjoyment, judgement
7. a t n — action, eating

Underline the suffix that you **cannot** add to the word in **bold**.

8. **origin**   al   ate   <u>able</u>   s
9. **act**   ive   or   <u>ist</u>   tion
10. **forgive**   able   ness   ing   <u>tion</u>

B WORD WORK

1. The same four-letter string is missing from all these words. Write it in.

   sh<u>ould</u>ers   b<u>ould</u>er   w<u>ould</u>   c<u>ould</u>

2. What do you notice?

   'ould' has two different sounds.

Add a prefix and/or a suffix to make a new word.

3. script <u>ure</u>   **Clue:** holy writings
4. <u>pre</u> script <u>ion</u>   **Clue:** for medicine
5. <u>post</u> script   **Clue:** PS
6. <u>in</u> script <u>ion</u>   **Clue:** on a gravestone
7. The root word **script** means <u>written</u>.

Write a definition of the word or words in **bold**.

8. **Score** along the dotted lines.
   score: mark with something sharp
9. He listened to **heavy metal**.
   heavy metal: a type of music
10. I searched the **web**.
    web: the worldwide web

PART A Focus
1–4: word order; punctuation
5–7: visual spelling strategies
8–10: adding suffixes

PART B Focus
1–2: common letter strings
3–7: root words
8–10: context-specific meanings

C SENTENCE WORK

Complete this sentence to make Joe sound

1. **happy:** "Listen to this," chuckled Joe, with a twinkle in his eye.
2. **shocked:** "Listen to this," gasped Joe, staring at the letter in amazement.
3. **worried:** "Listen to this," muttered Joe, with a furrowed brow.

Cross out the nouns and replace them with proper names.

4. ~~That player~~ plays for ~~that team~~.   Ben Earl, Woodfield Town
5. I saw ~~a woman~~ going into ~~a shop~~.   Madonna, M&S
6. ~~This man~~ is in charge of ~~this organisation~~.   Mr Jenkins, Sunshine Foods

Why has the writer used brackets?

7. Fold the corners into the centre (see Diagram 2).   To include a helpful note.
8. Nelson (1758–1805) was a famous sea admiral.   To include an extra piece of information.
9. Foxes live in many urban (built-up) areas.   To give a definition.
10. Sally (whom I never did trust) went straight to the teacher.   To add a personal comment.

PART C Focus
1–3: using dialogue; words chosen for effect
4–6: proper nouns for precision
7–10: uses of brackets

18   X DEFINITIVE ANSWER   X SAMPLE ANSWER

Section 2 Test 2

A WARM-UP

Rewrite the sentence, first as an imperative (I) and then as a question (Q).

The pizza is in the oven.

1. I: _Put the pizza in the oven._
2. Q: _Is the pizza in the oven?_

Make three words.

fit un ful ing ly

3. _unfit_
4. _fittingly_
5. _fitful_

Write three words that end with the suffix.

6. _govern_ ment   _docu_ ment   _orna_ ment
7. _hero_ ic   _com_ ic   _poet_ ic

Put the letters in order to make a word.

8. d n o s u — _sound_
9. e g h i w — _weigh_
10. e g h n o u — _enough_

PART A Focus
1–2: questions and imperatives
3–7: prefixes and suffixes
8–10: visual spelling strategies

B WORD WORK

Add the missing vowels.

1. e x c _e_ l l _e_ n t
2. s e v _e_ r _a_ l
3. d e f _i_ n _i_ t e

PART B Focus
1–3: unstressed vowels
4–7: homophones
8–10: word structure and meaning; adverbs

Read the words aloud. Underline the odd one out.

4. too two to <u>tow</u>
5. so sow <u>saw</u> sew
6. Why are the odd ones out different?
   They sound different.
7. What do you notice about the other words in each group?
   They are all homophones/sound the same but have different spellings and meanings.
8. Underline the root word.
   <u>peril</u>ously <u>triumph</u>antly

Write a definition.

9. **perilously:** _dangerously_
10. **triumphantly:** _as if the winner_

C SENTENCE WORK

Continue the sentence using one of these words.

who where which

1. Once there was a poor farmer _who had only one skinny cow._
2. There was once a faraway kingdom _where all the people were very sad._
3. They huddled round the fire, _which was fading fast._
4. George was a stonecutter _who lived in a little cottage on the edge of the wood._

Some words have been crossed out. Write new words that sound more formal.

5. They ~~got rid of~~ _disposed of_ the ~~stuff~~ _goods_.
6. They ~~got hold of~~ _seized_ the ~~gear~~ _equipment_.
7. He seemed ~~a bit shady~~ _somewhat untrustworthy_.

Underline the correct word of the three that appear in brackets.

8. There were once three (<u>sisters</u> / sister's / sisters').
9. The three (brothers / brother's / <u>brothers'</u>) home was tiny.
10. (Helens / <u>Helen's</u> / Helens') donkey trotted off down the road.

PART C Focus
1–4: using connectives
5–7: formal language
8–10: possessive apostrophes

Section 2 Test 3

A WARM-UP

Complete the sentence.

1. Dan did not speak although _everyone was waiting._
2. Dan did not speak until _the room was silent._
3. Dan did not speak in case _someone was listening._

Add one letter to make a new word.

4. hear — _shear_
5. word — _world_
6. wait — _waist_
7. favour — _flavour_

PART A Focus
1–3: using connectives
4–7: visual spelling strategies
8–9: spelling patterns
10: plural spelling rules

Add the same short word to complete all three longer words.

8. a v e r _age_   i m _age_   v i l l _age_
9. h a r b _our_   h _our_   f l _our_

10. Change the words into plurals.

| factory | _factories_ | marsh | _marshes_ |
| industry | _industries_ | valley | _valleys_ |

B WORD WORK

1. Add **full** or **ful**.

   full er   _full_ y   doubt _ful_   faith _ful_

2. What spelling pattern do you notice?

   When used as a suffix, 'ful' has one 'l'.

3. Add **all** or **al**.

   _al_ ways   _al_ most   _al_ ready   over _all_

4. What spelling pattern do you notice?

   When used as a prefix, 'al' has one 'l'.

Add prefixes and/or suffixes to make three new words.

5. lone — _alone, lonely, lonesome_
6. cover — _uncover, recover, discovery_
7. real — _unreal, really, reality_

Add the missing word to the well-known phrase.

8. as fit as _a fiddle_
9. as cool as _a cucumber_
10. as blind as _a bat_

PART B Focus
1–4: double and single consonants
5–7: word structure
8–10: idioms

C SENTENCE WORK

What a mess! You wouldn't believe it. Norma's cottage? More like Nor–mess cottage!

1. Underline the two words that best describe the style of this story.

   <u>chatty</u> formal warm <u>jokey</u> descriptive

Give three reasons to explain your choice.

2. _The questions and exclamations make it sound chatty._
3. _The shortened forms sound informal._
4. _The pun adds humour._

Complete these metaphors.

5. The river _is a shining ribbon trailing across the countryside._
6. His eyes _were giant headlights shining in the darkness._
7. Fog _is a thin veil over the world._

Cross out any unnecessary commas.

8. One night, as he lay asleep, under the stars, Angelo had, a dream.
9. For several minutes, the wizard looked, at him, in silence.
10. The old woman, hurriedly, hid the food, in the woodpile, hoping no-one, would look there.

PART C Focus
1–4: narrative style
5–7: metaphors
8–10: commas to mark phrases; clauses

Section 2 Test 4

A WARM-UP

Write a sentence using one of these words.

entirely relatively importantly

1. He was entirely wrong.
2. It was a relatively small increase.
3. More importantly, he won the cup.

4. Make six words using these letters only.

   o n t w

   own, town, ton, now, on, two

Remove one letter to make a new word.

5. beard — bear
6. monkey — money
7. through — though

PART A Focus
1–3: adverbs to clarify
4–7: visual spelling strategies
8–10: ible and able

Underline the correct spelling.

8. flexable flexeble <u>flexible</u>
9. reversable reverseble <u>reversible</u>
10. <u>forgivable</u> forgiveble forgivible

B WORD WORK

Underline the word that is **not** a real word.

1. autograph automobile <u>autonature</u>
2. microscope <u>microbitus</u> microphone
3. <u>telecut</u> telephone telescope

Write two homophones.

4. road — rode, rowed
5. you — ewe, yew
6. by — buy, bye
7. rain — rein, reign

PART B Focus
1–3: word roots
4–7: homophones
8–10: soft and hard c

Sort the words into two groups.

city collar cope cell case cub cycle cyst

8. soft c: city, cell, cycle, cyst
9. hard c: collar, cope, case, cub

10. What letters usually follow a soft **c**?

    'i', 'e' or 'y'

C SENTENCE WORK

Continue the sentence.

1. He stopped suddenly as if he'd been frozen.
2. Suddenly darkness descended as though a light had been switched off.
3. He would continue his search as long as the rain held off.
4. Amanda was the oldest sister as well as the most beautiful.

Sort the words into two groups that could be used to describe a character.

uncaring generous bold snivelling devious feeble dependable cheerful

5. appealing: generous, bold, dependable, cheerful
6. unappealing: uncaring, snivelling, devious, feeble

Underline the correct word of those that appear in brackets.

7. It was (<u>their</u> / there / they're) day off.
8. I believe (their / there / <u>they're</u>) away on holiday.
9. I hope (your / <u>you're</u>) coming.
10. I shall put this in (<u>your</u> / you're) folder.

PART C Focus
1–4: using connectives
5–6: words chosen for effect
7–10: possessive pronouns; using apostrophes

X DEFINITIVE ANSWER   X SAMPLE ANSWER

Section 2   Test 5

A   WARM-UP

Rewrite the sentence in a more formal way.

1 I ditched the rest.
   I disposed of the remainder.

2 The film was slated.
   The film was badly received.

3 The kids soon perked up.
   The children soon cheered up.

Change one letter to make a homophone. Write the new word and its meaning.

PART A Focus
1–3: formal and informal language
4–6: homophones
7–10: word structure

4 peek (a look)   _peak (the top)_

5 steel (a metal)   _steal (take)_

6 sun (a star)   _son (parent's boy)_

Add different endings to complete the three words.

7 pack _et_   pack _age_   pack _ing_

8 press _ing_   press _ure_   press _ed_

9 assist _ed_   assist _ant_ assist _ing_

10 stick _y_   stick _er_   stick _ing_

B   WORD WORK

1 What do the words have in common?
   glug buzz slosh pop
   They are onomatopoeic.

2 Add **ed** endings.
   glugged, buzzed, sloshed, popped

3 Write four more words of the type you identified in question 1.
   boom, creak, oink, zoom

Complete the word sum.

4 **collect** + **tion** = _collection_

5 **expand** + **sion** = _expansion_

6 **decide** + **sion** = _decision_

PART B Focus
1–3: onomatopoeia; rules for adding ed
4–8: adding tion and sion
9–10: antonyms

7 What do you notice?
   The **sion** words _end in 'd' or 'de'._

8 Write four more words ending with **tion**.
   attention, action, station, direction

Underline the antonym of the word in **bold**.

9 **prosperous**   wealthy <u>poor</u> affluent

10 **trustworthy**   <u>dishonest</u> reliable solid

C   SENTENCE WORK

Rewrite the sentence, rearranging the words, phrases and clauses and using the correct punctuation.

1 Everyone celebrated except Prince James when Princess Agnes was born.
   When Princess Agnes was born everyone celebrated – except Prince James.

2 Many years ago there lived a dragon named Jem in a kingdom by the sea.
   Many years ago, in a kingdom by the sea, there lived a dragon named Jem.

3 The doors flew open suddenly just as everyone was sitting down to eat.
   Just as everyone was sitting down to eat, the doors suddenly flew open.

Cross out the words that are wrong. Write them in correct Standard English.

4 I ~~seen~~ him pick up the book ~~what~~ was lying on the floor.   _saw, that_

5 I planted ~~them~~ bulbs and ~~done~~ some weeding.   _those, did_

6 They ~~was~~ not afraid although they did not have ~~no~~ shelter.   _were, any_

7 The man must ~~of took~~ the money ~~what~~ was on the table.   _have taken, that_

PART C Focus
1–3: reordering sentences
4–7: Standard English
8–10: noun selection; story genre

Add nouns to fit the type of story.

8 legend: _St George_ faced the _dragon_.

9 horror story: _Tim_ faced the _vampire_.

10 school story: _Mr Stern_ faced _the class_.

22   X DEFINITIVE ANSWER   X SAMPLE ANSWER

Section 2 Test 6

A WARM-UP

Continue the sentence.

1. She spoke as if <u>she knew someone was listening.</u>
2. He crouched down as though <u>trying to hide.</u>
3. They would remain there as long as <u>the King allowed.</u>

These root words are mixed up. Write them correctly.

megaman supercab miniphone

4. <u>megaphone</u>
5. <u>minicab</u>
6. <u>superman</u>

7. Write three words using the root word **super**.
   <u>supersonic, superstar, supermarket</u>

Add the missing letters.

Clue: use the name of a different family member to complete each word

8. h<u>au</u>n<u>t</u>ed
9. les<u>so</u>n
10. s<u>mother</u>

PART A Focus
1–3: using connectives
4–7: word roots
8–10: visual spelling strategies

B WORD WORK

1. Add **ing** to these onomatopoeic words.
   chug<u>ging</u>   hum<u>ming</u>   beep<u>ing</u>   snap<u>ping</u>

Write three onomatopoeic words that might describe the sounds made by

2. an old car: <u>rattle, creak, chug</u>
3. water: <u>splash, splosh, slosh</u>
4. animals: <u>oink, moo, quack</u>

5. Add the correct prefix.

   il im in ir

   <u>in</u> human   <u>ir</u> rational
   <u>il</u> logical   <u>im</u> polite

6. How do the prefixes change the word?
   <u>They make a word with the opposite meaning.</u>

Write another word beginning with the prefix.

7. in <u>visible</u>
8. ir <u>responsible</u>
9. il <u>legal</u>
10. im <u>possible</u>

PART B Focus
1: rules for adding ing
2–4: onomatopoeia
5–10: prefixes that change meaning

C SENTENCE WORK

Join the two sentences without using **and**.

1. Joe reached the top. He shouted down. <u>When Joe reached the top, he shouted down.</u>
2. He looked at the box. He wondered what was inside.
   <u>He looked at the box, wondering what was inside.</u>
3. The little goat trotted down the road. He munched a few leaves as he went.
   <u>The little goat trotted down the road, munching a few leaves as he went.</u>

PART C Focus
1–3: combining sentences
4–7: uses of dashes
8–10: Standard English

Why has the writer used a dash?

4. "If you don't want me to stay – I won't," sniffed Georgie. <u>To show a pause in speech.</u>
5. Everything returned to normal – well almost! <u>For dramatic effect and surprise.</u>
6. He couldn't walk any further – the pain was too bad. <u>To add extra information.</u>
7. five o'clock – meet Nikki <u>To help keep a note short.</u>

Cross out the words that are wrong. Write them in correct Standard English.

8. I ~~done~~ the shopping while you ~~was~~ asleep. <u>did, were</u>
9. If they ~~was~~ hungry they could help ~~theirselves~~ to the sandwiches. <u>were, themselves</u>
10. I could have ~~give~~ you ~~me~~ spare trainers. <u>given, my</u>

Section 2   Test 7

A   WARM-UP

Write two adverbs that give different effects.

1. He spoke ___nervously___ / ___confidently___ .
2. She reacted ___calmly___ / ___angrily___ .
3. ___Hurriedly___ / ___Carefully___ , he gathered the papers together.

4. The same five-letter string is missing from all these words. Write it in.

   d ___aught___ e r   t ___aught___   c ___aught___

Add a three-letter word to complete the longer word.

5. c r ___eat___ u r e
6. g r ___ace___ f u l
7. s t ___ran___ g e

Add a four-, five- or six-letter word to make a longer word.

8. i n ___flat___ a b l e
9. r e ___place___ m e n t
10. e n ___danger___ e d

PART A Focus
1–3: adverbs to clarify
4–7: letter strings; spelling strategies
8–10: word structure

B   WORD WORK

Add the correct 'shun' ending.

1. discuss ___ion___   confuse ___ion___
2. reduce ___tion___   collide ___sion___

PART B Focus
1–2: tion, sion and ssion
3–4: root words
5–10: meaning of homonyms

Write the root word and another word with the same root.

	Root word	Words with the same root
3	moist	moisture moisten
4	drama	dramatic dramatise

Write sentences showing the two different meanings of the word.

5. fan: He is a Leeds United fan.
6. fan: We need a fan to keep cool.
7. current: My current score is 10.
8. current: The wire carries a current.
9. overall: He did well overall.
10. overall: He wears an overall at work.

C   SENTENCE WORK

Expand the notes into a complete sentence.

1. **no sun = no life on Earth** — If there were no sun, there would be no life on Earth.
2. **hibernate – survive winter** — Some animals hibernate in order to survive winter.
3. **clouds = water drops** — Clouds are made up of millions of tiny drops of water.

Add words that give the two characters opposing characteristics. Write the name of the story type.

legend   fable   folk tale

4. The ladybird ___hurried___ and ___scurried___ . The grasshopper ___dozed___ in the sun.   ___fable___
5. Jon was ___sociable___ and ___cheerful___ . His wife was ___selfish___ and ___grumpy___ .   ___folk tale___
6. The Red Knight ___fought___ through the ___brambles___ . The Green Knight ___trembled___ nearby.   ___legend___

Underline the information that is **not** essential to the sentence. Add commas to separate it.

7. Neptune, <u>one of the gas giants</u>, is the eighth planet from the Sun.
8. Many stringed instruments, <u>such as the violin</u>, are played with a bow.
9. Hares, <u>like rabbits</u>, have long ears and powerful hind legs.
10. The iguanadon, <u>which was a herbivore</u>, was 10 metres long.

PART C Focus
1–3: sentences to explain or define
4–6: choosing words for effect; identifying story genre
7–10: commas to embed information

Section 2   Test 8

A   WARM-UP

Name the technique used here by the headline writer.

1. **Eggcellent news for Humpty!**
   Play on words.
2. **Wanda's wonderful woolly!**
   Alliteration.
3. **'I was framed' says art thief**
   Pun.
4. Write a headline about Bo Peep.
   Sheep mystery deepens

Add one letter to make the homophone.

5. **not**   Knot
6. **hole** whole

Add different endings to complete the three words.

7. child ren   child less   child like
8. pain ful   pain less   pain killer

Write the noun as a plural.

9. one wolf → two wolves
10. one goose → two geese

PART A Focus
1–4: headlines; word play
5–6: homophones
7–8: root words; suffixes
9–10: plurals

B   WORD WORK

Add **s** or **c** to complete the words.

1. de c ide   in c ident   in s tant   de c ent
2. c ircuit   c ertain   s alute   c ement
3. ra c e   fan c y   promi s e   i c e

PART B Focus
1–3: spellings with soft c
4–7: prefixes
8–10: onomatopoeia

Make opposites by adding the same prefix to all three words.

4. de mist   de compose   de frost
5. dis mount   dis connect   dis mantle
6. non -starter   non -drip   non -smoker
7. un equal   un healthy   un certain

Write three onomatopoeic words to suit each setting.

8. **building site**   clatter, thud, crash
9. **deserted house**   creak, squeak, click
10. **riverbank**   gurgle, plop, splash

C   SENTENCE WORK

Continue the sentence in the style of a traditional story.

1. And so a great banquet was held to celebrate the marriage of the Prince and Princess.
2. But on the third night , there was a scurrying and a scampering outside the door.
3. There was once a tiger who thought he was the King of the jungle.

What sort of answer does each question need: explanation, opinion, fact or description?

4. When was the King born?   fact
5. What did the thief look like?   description
6. Why are rain clouds grey?   explanation
7. What did you think of the film?   opinion

Underline the correct word of the two that appear in brackets.

8. Do you know (whose / **who's**) coming?
9. Do you know (**whose** / who's) book this is?
10. We (**were** / we're) on time, but now (were / **we're**) late.

PART C Focus
1–3: narrative style; sentence construction
4–7: question types
8–10: common confusions using apostrophes

X DEFINITIVE ANSWER   X SAMPLE ANSWER

Section 2   Test 9

A   WARM-UP

Rewrite each sentence to say **when**, **where** and **what for**.

1 He begged. _In the morning he went to his brother's house and begged for forgiveness._

2 He travelled. _For many years he travelled the world looking for the lost treasure._

Join the prefix to its meaning.

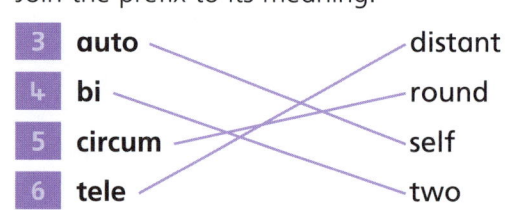

3 auto — distant
4 bi — round
5 circum — self
6 tele — two

(auto→self, bi→two, circum→round, tele→distant)

7 Write six words that start with **hand**.
handsome, handful, handiwork, handle, handcuffs, handshake

Add the missing vowels.

8 m_i_n_u_t_e_s
9 f_a_m_i_ly
10 J_a_n_u_a_ry

> **PART A Focus**
> 1–2: expanding sentences
> 3–6: meaning of common roots
> 7: word structure
> 8–10: unstressed vowels in common words

B   WORD WORK

1 Underline the words that begin with a soft **g**.
<u>gentle</u> gallop <u>gym</u> <u>geography</u> golf

2 Write three more words beginning with a soft **g**.
gerbil, giant, genius

3 Add the missing **c** or **s**.
o_c_ean   an_c_ient   ver_s_e

Underline the correct spelling.

4 dredfully   <u>dreadfully</u>   dreadfuly
5 furyous   furrious   <u>furious</u>
6 hurridly   <u>hurriedly</u>   huriedly

Write two antonyms for each word.

7 love — _hate, loathe_
8 good — _bad, poor_
9 soft — _hard, tough_

10 Underline the word that has no opposite.
happy   <u>red</u>   bright   little

> **PART B Focus**
> 1–3: soft g and soft c
> 4–6: spelling rules for adding suffixes
> 7–10: antonyms

C   SENTENCE WORK

Continue the sentence to explain why.

1 Every year thousands of trees are cut down _to be made into paper._
2 Water is essential to life on Earth _because plants and animals would die without it._
3 Yeast is often added to bread _in order to make the bread rise._
4 Myths are called traditional stories _because they are passed from generation to generation._

Rewrite the sentence, replacing the common noun in **bold** with a more descriptive noun phrase.

5 He saw **a man**. _He saw a strange little man with red hair._
6 **A woman** stood nearby. _An old woman with a woollen shawl stood nearby._
7 He saw **a man**. _He saw a police officer speaking into his radio._
8 **A woman** stood nearby. _A woman dressed in designer clothes stood nearby._

Add commas, full stops and capital letters to make these texts make sense.

9 Holding onto the side, he kicked his legs. T_he boat moved.
10 Tess smiled. H_er mother, Lucy, laughed out loud.

> **PART C Focus**
> 1–4: expanding sentences to explain
> 5–8: expanded noun phrases
> 9–10: commas and full stops

26   X DEFINITIVE ANSWER   X SAMPLE ANSWER

Section 2   Test 10

A WARM-UP

Emily admits she was wrong.

Rewrite the sentence as

1. **past tense:** Emily admitted she was wrong.
2. **future tense:** Emily will admit she was wrong.
3. **direct speech:** "I was wrong," admitted Emily.
4. **an order:** Admit it, Emily – you were wrong.
5. **a question:** Will Emily admit she was wrong?

6. Write the verbs in the past tense.

   envy — envied
   spray — sprayed
   occupy — occupied

PART A Focus
1–5: verb tenses; sentence types; punctuation
6: spelling rules for adding ed
7–10: spelling strategies

Add the missing syllable or syllables.

7. im **por** tant   *Clue:* vital
8. dis **gus** ting   *Clue:* horrible
9. a **ston** ish **ment**   *Clue:* surprise
10. pre **dic** tion   *Clue:* forecast

B WORD WORK

1. Add the missing letter.

   tempt **a** tion   em **o** tion
   poll **u** tion   compl **e** tion
   pos **i** tion

2. Add the same ending to all three words.

   Clue: occupations

   opti **cian**   electri **cian**   mathemati **cian**

   Write two more occupations with the same ending.

   3. musician   4. magician

PART B Focus
1–4: tion and cian
5–10: common roots

Write a definition.

5. **transform:** change completely
6. **translate:** write in a different language
7. **transport:** move, carry

8. Write four more words with the root **trans**.
   transplant, transfer, transmit, transfix

Add the root that will complete all three words.

9. **inter** national   **inter** act   **inter** net
10. **tech** nology   **tech** nical   **tech** nique

C SENTENCE WORK

Rewrite the sentence, changing the word order as you do so.

1. The Duchess looked down sadly on the little town from up in her tower.
   From up in her tower, the Duchess looked down sadly on the little town.
2. The film star came through the door accompanied by two men.
   Through the door, accompanied by two men, came the film star.
3. He ran to the door immediately on hearing the footsteps.
   On hearing the footsteps, he immediately ran to the door.

Use onomatopoeic words to complete the sentence.

PART C Focus
1–3: reordering sentences
4–7: using onomatopoeia
8–10: colons, brackets and dashes

4. The machine began to **judder** and **rumble**.
5. The geese **honked**, the cows **mooed** and the horses **neighed**. What a noise!
6. Alone in the forest, I listened to the **swish** of the wind and the **creak** of the branches.
7. The city **buzzed** with the **hum** of traffic and the **chatter** of people.

Continue the sentence after the punctuation mark.

8. Many objects are made from wood: tables, shelves, cupboards and pencils.
9. The rock is porous (full of holes).
10. The door slammed – they were trapped!

Section 2 Test 11

A WARM-UP

1 Continue the sentence so that it is at least 25 words long.

Suddenly he stopped _chopping the wood and looked around him, as if waiting for someone or something to appear out of the shadows of the night._

Write the antonym.

2 forward — _backward_
3 increase — _decrease_
4 fearful — _fearless_

PART A Focus
1: extending sentences
2–4: forming antonyms
5–6: word construction; word roots
7–10: spelling strategies

5 Write four words that start with **light**.
lightly, lighten, lighter, lightning

6 Write four words that end with **light**.
moonlight, sunlight, starlight, daylight

Add the missing letters.
Clue: use the name of a different part of the body to complete each word

7 c h _arm_ i n g
8 s u r _face_
9 s _ear_ c h
10 w _heel_

B WORD WORK

Underline the correct spelling.

1 germ   jerm   gurm
2 justise   justice   gustice
3 gorjous   gorgous   gorgeous

PART B Focus
1–3: soft g and soft c
4–6: word meanings; context
7–10: meaning of common idioms

Write a definition of the word in **bold**, found on a food safety poster.

4 **hygienic:** _clean, free of germs_
5 **disposable:** _throw-away_
6 **contaminated:** _infected_

In your own words, rewrite the phrase in **bold**.

7 If you **put your foot in it** you _make a blunder._
8 If you **put your feet up** you _take a rest._
9 If you **put your foot down** you _go faster/insist/say no._
10 If you **have your feet on the ground** you _are practical._

C SENTENCE WORK

Combine the three sentences into one.

1 The man had magic shoes. The man wore the shoes every day. The shoes wore out.
The man had magic shoes, which he wore every day until they wore out.

2 Ursula sold all her hats. She kept one hat. This one hat was Ursula's favourite.
Ursula sold all her hats except one, which was her favourite.

3 Out came an old man. The old man walked down the path. The path led to the village.
Out came an old man who walked down the path leading to the village.

Add appropriate nouns and adjectives.

4 Some jellyfish have _tentacles_ that can give a _painful sting_.
5 Crocodiles are _large reptiles_ found in _tropical regions_.
6 Mercury is a _small planet_ covered with _craters_.
7 A frog's skin is _smooth_, while a toad's is _rough_.

Underline the correct word of the three that appear in brackets.

8 There are two doctors. This is the (doctors / doctor's / doctors') surgery.
9 That is the home (teams / team's / teams') dressing room.
10 That is the (childrens / children's / childrens') playground.

PART C Focus
1–3: sentence formation
4–7: nouns and adjectives in non-fiction
8–10: possessive apostrophes

Section 2   Test 12

A WARM-UP
Complete the sentence.
1. Only as the clock _struck thirteen, did they realise something was wrong._
2. Then, from far and near, _people began to arrive in the marketplace._
3. By recycling, _we can help to save energy and raw materials._
4. Write the verbs in the past tense.

   flop _flopped_ **cram** _crammed_
   plead _pleaded_ **shrug** _shrugged_

Write three words that start with
5. **over:** _overcast, overdue, overall_
6. **out:** _outside, outlaw, outline_

Add the missing syllable.
Clue: types of writing
7. ex _pla_ n a t i o n
8. p e r _sua_ s i v e
9. i n _struc_ t i o n s
10. n a r _ra_ t i v e

PART A Focus
1–3: sentence construction
4: past tense; rules for adding ed
5–6: root words
7–10: spelling strategies

B WORD WORK
Add a word before or after the hyphen.
1. e- _mail_   x- _ray_
2. free- _range_   free- _wheel_
3. _low_ -energy   _eco_ -friendly
4. _sugar_ -free   _disease_ -free

Cross out the words that are wrong. Write the correct spellings.
5. The ~~caive~~ was ~~cramed~~ with ~~emralds~~.
   cave, crammed, emeralds
6. A ~~terrable~~ monster ~~garded~~ the ~~enterance~~.
   terrible, guarded, entrance

PART B Focus
1–4: hyphenated words
5–6: common spelling patterns
7–10: subject-specific word meanings

Write a definition of the word in **bold**, found in an art gallery.
7. **landscape:** _a picture of scenery_
8. **portrait:** _a picture of a person_

Write a definition of the word in **bold**, found in a word-processing program.
9. **landscape:** _page set out across ways_
10. **portrait:** _page set out downwards_

C SENTENCE WORK
Add a phrase or clause that gives extra information.
1. The man, _who was carrying the heavy sack_, climbed out of the window.
2. And so, _thanks to Prince Alfonso_, the land of Safara was free once more.
3. Vitamin C, _which is found in fresh fruit and vegetables_, helps to repair wounds.
4. Queen Victoria, _who became queen in 1837_, reigned for 63 years.

She peeked inside. And what do you think she saw?
5. Why does the story writer use this question? _To make readers wonder._

Write three similar questions.
6. _What should she do now?_
7. _Where was he?_
8. _What if the thief was hiding there?_

Reporter: Amy, is it true that you are going to live in America?
Amy Starlet: No comment.

PART C Focus
1–4: embedding a phrase or clause
5–8: story style; questions
9–10: direct and reported speech

9. Write the complete text as reported speech.
   Amy Starlet refused to comment on rumours of a move to America.
10. Write the reporter's question as direct speech in a story.
    "Amy, is it true that you're going to live in America?" quizzed a reporter.

Remind the pupil to complete Section 2 of the Progress chart on page 46 of the workbook.

Schofield & Sims English Skills 4

Section 2 Writing task assessment sheet: The tortoise and the hare

Name	Class/Set
Teacher's name	Date

Sentence structure and punctuation

	Always/often	Sometimes	Never
Uses varied sentence length (e.g., short for pace and impact; long for description)			
Sentences shaped for variety and effect (e.g., ordering of phrases, adverbs, clauses)			
Uses adverbs, phrases and clauses to add detail			
Uses a range of connectives to link ideas			
Uses tense appropriately			
Demarcates sentences accurately (no comma splice)			
Sets direct speech on new line, with speech marks			
Uses commas to mark phrases and clauses			
Uses apostrophes correctly			
Shows understanding of other punctuation (e.g., dash)			

Composition and effect

Details chosen for appeal to reader (e.g., humour)			
Story shaped into paragraphs, with shifts in time and place clearly signalled			
Explicit or implied narrative viewpoint is maintained			
Language (including adverbs) chosen for effect			
Expanded noun phrases and adjectives add detail			
Traditional story style includes questions, repetition and speech-like connectives			

Spelling

Phonically regular words are correctly spelt			
Consonant spelling patterns correctly applied (e.g., soft **c** and **g**; single and double consonants)			
Common letter strings correctly spelt (e.g., **ough**, **tch**)			
Tricky medium-frequency words correct, including those with unstressed vowels			
Applies rules for adding prefixes and suffixes			
Applies rules for forming plurals			
Applies rules for adding verb endings			
Common homophones correct			

From: **English Skills 4 Answers** by Carol Matchett (ISBN 978 07217 1184 3). Copyright © Schofield & Sims Ltd, 2011. Published by Schofield & Sims Ltd, Dogley Mill, Fenay Bridge, Huddersfield HD8 0NQ, UK (www.schofieldandsims.co.uk). **This page may be photocopied for use within your school or institution only.**

Schofield & Sims English Skills 4
Section 2 Completed proofreading task: Fruity fruit salad

Name	Class/Set
Teacher's name	Date

You could make this colourful fruit salad for a special family occasion. It's really delicious.

1. Peel, core and chop the apples into wedges and immediately toss them in lemon juice. (Warning! Be careful when using knives. Always ask an adult to help.)

2. Deseed the grapes, halve the strawberries and break several satsumes into segments.

3. Place all the fruit in a large bowl, together with any juice you have collected during the preparation.

4. Carefully measure out 100ml of orange juice and pour over the fruit to moisten it. Stir gently with a wooden spoon.

5. Slice two kiwi fruit and keep these for decoration.

6. Leave for about 20 minutes – just long enough to let the flavours combine. Once ready, serve to your guests and let everyone enjoy it!

Section 2 tasks summary

From: **English Skills 4 Answers** by Carol Matchett (ISBN 978 07217 1184 3). Copyright © Schofield & Sims Ltd, 2011. Published by Schofield & Sims Ltd, Dogley Mill, Fenay Bridge, Huddersfield HD8 0NQ, UK (www.schofieldandsims.co.uk). **This page may be photocopied for use within your school or institution only.**

Section 3   Test 1

A   WARM-UP

Write four sentences using these words only.

into   swiftly   the   rode   he   night

1. He rode swiftly into the night.
2. Into the night, he rode swiftly.
3. Swiftly, he rode into the night.
4. Into the night, he swiftly rode.

Add one letter to make a new word.

5. plant — planet
6. chef — chief
7. cover — clover

PART A Focus
1–4: reordering sentences
5–7: visual spelling strategies
8–10: suffixes

Add the same suffix to complete all three words.

8. poison**ous**   prosper**ous**   hazard**ous**
9. miser**able**   respect**able**   suit**able**
10. tropic**al**   post**al**   nature**al**

B   WORD WORK

Complete the word sum.

1. shovel + ing = shovelling
2. red + ish = reddish
3. fit + est = fittest
4. What spelling rule did you use?
   Double the final consonant when adding the suffix.

Add the correct prefix.

in   im   il   ir

5. **im** possible   **il** legal
6. **ir** responsible   **in** accurate
7. All these prefixes mean not.

PART B Focus
1–4: spelling rules for adding suffixes
5–7: less common prefixes
8–10: using word roots to work out meaning

What does the adjective tell you?

8. an **aquatic** animal
   The animal lives in water.
9. a **futuristic** car
   The car is ahead of its time.
10. stores **nationwide**
    The stores are all over the country.

C   SENTENCE WORK

Rewrite the three sentences as one. Do this in three different ways.

It was snowing. Mick stayed at home. He stayed snug by the fire.

1. As it was snowing, Mick stayed at home, snug by the fire.
2. It was snowing so Mick stayed at home, snug by the fire.
3. Mick stayed at home, snug by the fire, because it was snowing.

PART C Focus
1–3: forming sentences
4–6: constructing sentences for a report
7–10: punctuating sentences accurately

Rewrite the sentence so that it sounds as it would in a report.

4. The monkey kept leaping around.   Monkeys are agile animals.
5. Some things stick to the magnet and some jump away.
   Some objects are attracted to the magnet while others are repelled.
6. The floppy-eared elephant swings his trunk sadly.
   Elephants are huge animals with large ears and a long trunk.

Add commas, full stops and capital letters to make the meaning clear.

7. Little Jimmy was fed up, too. He sat on the floor, refusing to move.
8. In less than a minute, the entire village vanished. Yes, vanished into thin air.
9. As the Prince rode, he sang to raise his spirits. Of course, he hoped no-one would hear.
10. Amazed at his good fortune, Jas won tickets for the Final. He was so lucky!

Section 3   Test 2

A   WARM-UP

Complete the sentence to give a different view of the character.

1. "I know," __said__ Abby, __comforting him.__
2. "I know," __screamed__ Abby, __banging her fists on the table.__
3. "I know," __exclaimed__ Abby, __excitedly.__

Read the title and guess the type of story.

4. The Enchanted Piper — __traditional__
5. Tiddles – the Supercat! — __humorous__
6. The Curse of Bleak Towers — __horror__

7. Make three words.

tele photo ic graph

__telegraph, graphic, photographic__

Draw a line to join the root to its meaning.

8. tele — distant
9. graph — to write
10. photo — light

PART A Focus
1–3: words chosen for effect
4–6: story genre
7–10: common roots

B   WORD WORK

Add the same two letters to complete both words.

1. fact **o r** y   categ **o r** y
2. int **e r** est   lit **e r** acy

Add a suffix to the word in **bold**. Use the new word to complete the sentence.

3. He was a **king** without a __kingdom__.
4. We all need the __friendship__ of a **friend**.
5. She paid her __membership__ fee and became a **member** of the club.
6. The **hero** behaved __heroically__.

Use a root word and the suffix **tion** to complete the sentence.

pollute irrigate purify consume

7. Factory waste can cause water __pollution__.
8. __Purification__ makes water safe to drink.
9. __Irrigation__ is vital for crops to grow.
10. Find ways to cut water __consumption__.

PART B Focus
1–2: unstressed vowels
3–6: root words and suffixes
7–10: the suffix tion; spelling patterns

C   SENTENCE WORK

We can all help to save the planet, starting right now.

Rewrite the sentence as

1. an imperative: __Start right now – save the planet.__
2. an exclamation: __Save the planet – starting NOW!__
3. a rhetorical question: __Shouldn't we all be doing our bit to save the planet?__

Write **definite** or **possibility** beside each statement.

4. I will do that tomorrow. — __definite__
5. I might do that tomorrow. — __possibility__
6. Maybe I'll do that tomorrow. — __possibility__
7. I could do that tomorrow. — __possibility__

Add an extra piece of information about the character, with a comma before and after.

8. Simeon __, Sam's evil brother,__ was waiting.
9. Mr Sprott __, the schoolmaster,__ glared at the young urchin.
10. Marianne __, who was sixteen years old,__ liked living in the old house.

PART C Focus
1–3: sentence types
4–7: modal verbs
8–10: commas to embed phrases and clauses

X DEFINITIVE ANSWER   X SAMPLE ANSWER

Section 3　Test 3

A　WARM-UP

Complete the sentence in different ways.

1. He hurried on as if __he were late.__

2. He hurried on in case __the robbers caught up.__

Add the same four-letter word to complete all the longer words.

3. i n t e __rest__
4. __rest__ a u r a n t
5. a r __rest__ e d

PART A Focus
1–2: using a variety of connectives
3–5: visual spelling strategies
6–7: homophones
8–10: suffixes

Use a pair of homophones to complete the sentence.

6. After a w __eek__, he was too w __eak__ to move.
7. The lady m __ade__ her m __aid__ carry the bags.

Add the same suffix to all three words.

8. awe __some__　　fear __some__　　hand __some__
9. like __wise__　　length __wise__　　clock __wise__
10. back __ward__　　home __ward__　　on __ward__

B　WORD WORK

Write the word split into syllables.
Draw a ring round the vowel that is difficult to hear and makes the word tricky to spell.

1. different　　dif / f(e)r / ent
2. desperate　　des / p(e)r / ate
3. definite　　def / (i) / nite

Write the verb that comes from the noun.

4. knee → to __kneel__
5. television → to __televise__
6. class → to __classify__
7. wide → to __widen__
8. editor → to __edit__

PART B Focus
1–3: unstressed vowels; spelling strategies
4–8: word formation
9–10: words with more than one meaning

Write two definitions.

9. shed: __to drop or throw off__
10. shed: __a simple building or shack__

C　SENTENCE WORK

Which story is for 4–6 year olds and which is for 7–10 year olds?

1. So Jack swapped Daisy the cow for a little bag of magic beans. __4–6 year olds__
2. So Jack (the twit) gave away the cow for a pile of (supposedly) magic beans. __7–10 year olds__

Give a reason for your answer.

3. The first story __uses simpler language and sentence construction.__
4. The second story __plays with the original one and has a more grown-up style.__

Write three words that would sound correct if used to fill the gap.

5. He walked _____ the wall.　　__on, by, along__
6. The book was _____ the desk.　　__in, on, under__
7. We had pizza _____ the film.　　__before, after, during__

PART C Focus
1–4: identifying text features for different readers
5–8: prepositions
9–10: possessive apostrophes

8. Underline the word type that identifies the words you have chosen.

   nouns　pronouns　**prepositions**

Add the apostrophes to this magic spell.

9. Mix the spots from four leopards' coats with two wasps' stings and a peacock's feather.
10. Sprinkle with the dust from six butterflies' wings and the shine from a unicorn's horn.

Section 3   Test 4

A   WARM-UP

Add a phrase or a clause to the start of the sentence.

1 _Stranded in the desert,_ the men were hungry.

2 _Because there was a famine,_ the men were hungry.

Write four onomatopoeic words.

3 cl _ick_   cl _op_   cl _atter_   cl _unk_

4 sl _am_   sl _osh_   sl _urp_   sl _op_

5 cr _eak_   cr _ackle_   cr _oak_   cr _unch_

Add the correct 'shun' ending and write the word.

6 **music**   _musician_

7 **collide**   _collision_

8 **create**   _creation_

9 **possess**   _possession_

10 **imagine**   _imagination_

PART A Focus
1–2: sentence construction
3–5: onomatopoeia
6–10: 'shun' endings

B   WORD WORK

1 Underline the long vowel sound.
   p**ie** v**ei**l v**ie**w sh**ie**ld
   p**ie**r r**ei**n f**ie**ry th**ei**r

PART B Focus
1–7: ei and ie spellings
8: word structure; prefixes and suffixes
9–10: subject-specific words

2 What do you notice?
   The letters 'ie' and 'ei' can make different sounds.

Sort the words into four groups.

3 **ee sound:** _shield, pier_

4 **i sound:** _pie, fiery_

5 **long a sound:** _veil, rein_

6 **other sounds:** _view, their_

7 How are the long **a** sounds spelt?
   With 'ei' rather than 'ie'.

8 Write four words using the root word **act**.
   actor, enact, active, activate

Write a definition of the word **conductor**, as found in

9 **a music book:** _leader of an orchestra_

10 **a science book:** _a material that conducts heat or electricity_

C   SENTENCE WORK

Rewrite the sentence so that it gives the same information, but as a **possibility**, not a definite fact.

1 It will be a better day tomorrow.   _It could be a better day tomorrow._

2 In the future we will drive electric cars.   _In the future we might drive electric cars._

Rewrite the sentence so that it gives the same information, but sounds more **definite**, rather than a possibility.

3 Your money could make a difference.   _Your money will make all the difference._

4 Your efforts might help save the planet.   _Your efforts will help save the planet._

Add powerful verbs to describe the actions of

5 **a hero:** He _brandished_ his sword, _leapt_ onto the white stallion and _galloped_ away.

6 **a wild animal:** It _reared_ up and _snarled_, _clawing_ at the air.

7 **a fire:** It _raged_ through the wood, _consuming_ the trees and _striding_ ever closer.

Add the punctuation to these headlines.

8 Merlin's the name – magic's his game!

9 Is the polar bear's Arctic world about to melt?

10 Pupils' art on display

PART C Focus
1–4: modal verbs
5–7: using powerful verbs for dramatic effect
8–10: punctuation

X DEFINITIVE ANSWER   X SAMPLE ANSWER

Section 3 Test 5

A WARM-UP

Write three sentences (S), a question (Q) and an imperative (I) using these words only.

you do better should really

1. S: *You should really do better.*
2. S: *You should do better, really.*
3. S: *Really, you should do better.*
4. Q: *Should you do better really?*
5. I: *Do better!*

Read aloud the list of words. Listen to their sounds. Underline the odd one out.

6. pour your <u>flour</u> tour
7. daughter <u>laughter</u> slaughter
8. rein veil <u>either</u> weigh

PART A Focus
1–5: word order; sentence type
6–8: letter strings with different sounds
9–10: words with more than one antonym

Underline two antonyms of the word in **bold**.

9. **slow** <u>rapid</u> laze <u>brisk</u> dawdle
10. **light** <u>dim</u> <u>weighty</u> joyful pale

B WORD WORK

Use a different three-letter word to complete each longer word.

Clue: each word starts with p

1. c o m *pan* y
2. h o s *pit* a l
3. How does breaking words down like this help you to spell them?
   It helps you to remember the unstressed vowels.

PART B Focus
1–3: unstressed vowels; spelling strategies
4–7: less-common prefixes
8–10: subject-specific words

These prefixes mean **not**.
Write two words that begin with each one.

4. ir *irregular, irrational*
5. il *illegible, illegal*
6. ir is added if *the root begins with 'r'.*
7. il is added if *the root begins with 'l'.*

Give a definition of the word in **bold**, found in notes for a design and technology project.

8. **reinforced** frame: *made stronger*
9. **mouldable** materials: *able to be shaped*
10. **compressed** material: *squashed down*

C SENTENCE WORK

Complete the sentence.

1. Along the riverbank, *people were waiting for the first boat to appear.*
2. During the night, *the old lady slept soundly.*
3. At the station, *Sergeant Green was waiting.*

PART C Focus
1–3: prepositional phrases
4–9: identifying text types
10: punctuating sentences

Write the text type that each text is taken from. Give a reason to support your answer.

Press the standby button on the remote control.

4. From: *an instruction manual.*
5. Reason: *It starts with an imperative.*

Clearly, we must stop this from happening!

6. From: *persuasive writing.*
7. Reason: *It tries to persuade.*

Rome, the capital city of Italy, stands on the banks of the River Tiber.

8. From: *a report or information text.*
9. Reason: *It gives factual information.*

Add two commas and a dash so that this sentence makes sense.

10. When he heard this, Joe began to laugh – not because it was funny, but because he was relieved to find that no-one knew the truth.

Section 3   Test 6

A   WARM-UP

Complete the sentence in two ways.

1. In the cold morning air, she shivered and pulled her coat around her.
2. Feeling a little anxious, she shivered despite the sunshine.

PART A Focus
1–2: sentence formation
3–6: spelling strategies
7–10: words from other languages

Add the missing syllables.

3. de f e n c e less   **Clue:** vulnerable, weak, frail
4. dis g u s t ed   **Clue:** shocked
5. m e s sen ger   **Clue:** one who carries a message
6. en d a n ger   **Clue:** to risk, threaten

Complete these words from other languages.

7. s p a g hetti   **Clue:** food (Italian)
8. k a r aoke   **Clue:** entertainment (Japanese)
9. g u i tar   **Clue:** musical instrument (Spanish)
10. d u n garees   **Clue:** clothing (Hindi)

B   WORD WORK

Add two more words with similar spellings.

1. cinema circle   circus, civil
2. cereal celebrity   centre, certain
3. gentle germ   general, generous
4. cycle Cyprus   cymbal, cylinder

5. Add the same prefix to all these words.
   Clue: it means **not**
   im possible   im patient
   im mature   im mobile

6. What do you notice about the root words?
   They begin with 'm' or 'p'.

Write the opposite of these maths terms.

7. **ascending**   descending
8. **positive**   negative
9. **probable**   improbable
10. **maximum**   minimum

PART B Focus
1–4: spelling patterns; soft c and g
5–6: the prefix im
7–10: opposites; subject-specific terms

C   SENTENCE WORK

Use the connectives to make a case for a Walking Bus scheme.

A Walking Bus scheme has many advantages.

1. For example, it would help to solve the parking problems outside the school gates.
2. Indeed, it would solve many traffic congestion problems around the school.
3. In addition, it would cut down on harmful pollution.
4. Furthermore, everyone taking part would be much fitter.

Sort these prepositional phrases into different types.

down the street, at midnight, to the cinema, during assembly, at school, between the gates, on Tuesday, after tea, in the shop, on top of the hill, over the fence, towards the hall

5. Showing time: at midnight, during assembly, on Tuesday, after tea
6. Showing position: at school, between the gates, in the shop, on top of the hill
7. Showing direction: down the street, to the cinema, over the fence, towards the hall

Add the punctuation to this dialogue.

8. "I'm 'ungry," moaned the monster, rubbing his stomach.
9. "You've just had breakfast," sighed Jim.
10. "Still 'ungry," moaned the monster. "Very 'ungry."

PART C Focus
1–4: connectives in arguments
5–7: classifying prepositions
8–10: punctuating direct speech; using apostrophes

X DEFINITIVE ANSWER   X SAMPLE ANSWER

Section 3   Test 7

A   WARM-UP

Try walking instead of using the car.

Present this idea as

1. an imperative: Don't use the car. Walk instead.
2. a question: Do you always use the car? Could you walk instead?
3. a slogan: Use your feet, not the car!

Split the word to show the prefix, root and suffix.

4. description — de / script / ion
5. unoriginal — un / origin / al
6. informal — in / form / al

Add a word after the hyphen.

7. hi- tech
8. dog- lover
9. problem- solving
10. in- built

PART A Focus
1–3: sentence types
4–6: word structure
7–10: hyphens; compound words

B   WORD WORK

Add **ei** or **ie** to make the long **ee** sound.

1. p ie rce   gr ie f
2. c ei ling   conc ei ted
3. What spelling rule did you use?
   'i' before 'e' except after 'c'.

Add the correct suffix. Make sure the word is spelt correctly.

ism   ity

4. hero ism   generous ity
5. sincere ity   tour ism
6. Write the words that name special qualities a person might have.
   heroism, generosity, sincerity

Write **formal** or **informal** beside each word or phrase.

7. stuck-up   informal
8. arrogant   formal
9. understand   formal
10. get it   informal

PART B Focus
1–3: spelling patterns ie and ei
4–6: less common suffixes
7–10: formal and informal synonyms

C   SENTENCE WORK

This text is from a magazine. Is it written for 4–6 year olds, 7–10 year olds or adults?

1. Get fit for summer, the world's hottest destinations and feel-good food. — adults
2. Full of mind-boggling facts, awesome activities and cool creations. — 7–10 year olds
3. Play new games and join in the fun with Moppy and Sam. — 4–6 year olds

Rewrite the sentence in a way that might appeal to 9–11 year olds.

4. Read about clever new inventions. — Explore incredible inventions and glorious gizmos.
5. Learn how you can help save the planet. — Go green! Learn how to save planet Earth!
6. Find out a lot about bats. — We all go bats about bats!

Use a dash to add information to the end of the sentence.

7. Don't throw newspapers away – recycle them instead.
8. Spiders live in many different places – including your home!

Use commas to embed extra information within the sentence.

9. William Shakespeare, the famous playwright, is well known all over the world.
10. The pyramids, which are the tombs of the pharaohs, are amazing buildings.

PART C Focus
1–6: writing for different readers
7–10: dashes and commas

Section 3 Test 8

A WARM-UP

Complete this sentence using different prepositional phrases.

1. Oliver waited _by the entrance._
2. Oliver waited _until midnight._
3. Oliver waited _with his mother._
4. Oliver waited _under the clock._

Add a homophone to complete the joke.

5. **Question:** Which vegetable can sink a boat?
   Clue: it's long, green and white
   Answer: A l_e_ _e_ _k_ !
6. **Waiter:** It's b_e_ _a_ _n_ soup, sir.
7. **Customer:** I don't care what it's b_e_ _e_ _n_ before, what is it now?

PART A Focus
1–4: prepositional phrases
5–7: homophones
8–10: acronyms; abbreviations

Write the meaning of the letters.

8. CD — _compact disk_
9. ROM — _read only memory_
10. pc — _personal computer_

B WORD WORK

Add the missing vowels. Draw a ring round the vowel sound that is difficult to hear.

1. e_a_ s_(i)_ l y
2. b u s _(i)_ n e s s
3. d _e_ _a_ f _(e)_ n i n g
4. w i d _(e)_ n i n g

PART B Focus
1–4: spelling strategies; unstressed vowels
5–6: adding suffixes
7–8: word classes
9–10: root words

Add a suffix and write the new word.

ise ify

5. magnet — _magnetise_
6. sign — _signify_

7. Underline the word type that best describes the root words above.
   <u>nouns</u> adjectives verbs

8. Underline the word type that best describes the new words above.
   nouns adjectives <u>verbs</u>

Write the noun that is linked to the adjective.

9. strong — _strength_
10. clear — _clarity_

C SENTENCE WORK

Continue the sentence as

1. **a traditional tale:** She came to _a castle of sparkling marble, hidden deep in the dark forest._
2. **a fantasy:** She came to _a giant metal cliff, which suddenly opened like a huge sliding door._
3. **a mystery story:** She came to _the end of the corridor, still searching for the hidden passage._

Rewrite the sentence in a more formal way.

4. I think a new leisure centre would be really cool. _Many local people believe that a new leisure centre would benefit the community._
5. There's not much else we can do. _There are no real alternatives._
6. We asked lots of people and nearly everyone said it would be great. _A recent survey shows widespread support for the idea._

PART C Focus
1–3: adapting sentences to story genre
4–6: using a formal style
7–10: using apostrophes

Put a tick if the apostrophe is used correctly. Put a cross if it is not. Explain your answer.

7. India's monsoon season ✓ _The monsoon season belongs to India._
8. No-ones' sure. ✗ _It should be 'no-one's', which is the shortened form of 'no-one is'._
9. "Where are you goin' then, laddy?" he asked. ✓ _'goin'' is a shortened form of 'going'._
10. Six tree's were chopped down. ✗ _'trees' is a plural, not a possessive noun._

| ✗ DEFINITIVE ANSWER | ✗ SAMPLE ANSWER |

39

Section 3 Test 9

A WARM-UP

Write three sentences, each one using the word **flat** in a different way.

flat parcel

1. The parcel was delivered to her flat.
2. The parcel was flat and square.
3. She sounded flat so I sent a parcel to cheer her up.

Use a different four-letter word to complete each longer word.

Clue: each word starts with **t**

4. d e _term_ i n e d
5. p r o _test_ e d
6. a t _tent_ i o n

PART A Focus
1–3: forming sentences
4–6: spelling strategies
7–10: puns; word play

Use the word to make up a pun or a word-play phrase.

7. peas — peas and quiet
8. tea — the big teas
9. cat — it's a cat-astrophe
10. snow — snow joke

B WORD WORK

Add three different suffixes and write the new words.

1. strange — strange<u>ly</u>, strang(er), strang(est)
2. tune — tun(ing) tun(ed), tune<u>less</u>
3. use — use<u>ful</u>, use<u>less</u>, us(er)

4. Draw a ring round the vowel suffixes. Then underline the consonant suffixes.
5. What pattern do you notice for adding suffixes to words ending with **e**?
   Keep the 'e' when adding consonant suffixes. Drop the 'e' when adding vowel suffixes.

Underline the correct word of the two that appear in brackets.

6. It was a ten (story / <u>storey</u>) building.
7. Blood contains red and white (<u>cells</u> / sells).
8. A (vain / <u>vein</u>) carries blood to the heart.

Add the missing part of the word.

9. advert_isement_
10. _aero_ plane

PART B Focus
1–5: spelling patterns; adding suffixes
6–8: homophones; subject-specific words
9–10: shortened words

C SENTENCE WORK

Use the dash to add a comment that makes the sentence sound more informal.

1. Miss Edgar was very angry — there was steam coming out of her ears!
2. Mum took Nikki's side — as usual.
3. It rained every day of our holiday — what a surprise!
4. We are going to win the league this year — I hope.

Sort the connectives into two groups.

on the other hand, certainly, however, clearly, furthermore, in contrast

5. **Making a case in favour:** certainly, clearly, furthermore
6. **Giving an opposing view:** on the other hand, however, in contrast
7. Write three more connectives that you might use to put the case **for** something.
   moreover, also, after all

PART C Focus
1–4: using dashes in informal writing
5–7: using connectives in discussion texts
8–10: speech marks and apostrophes

Add punctuation and capital letters.

8. "Don't!" cried Cyril. "Whatever you do, don't turn round."
9. Mr Jenkins, a 26-year-old plumber, told our reporter, "I didn't see the bus until it was too late."
10. Jack Spelling's book begins with the line: "Humphrey Norton's life was a mess."

Section 3   Test 10

A WARM-UP

1. Write an acrostic poem about rain.
   R _acing raindrops,_
   A _lways pouring,_
   I _n gutters, drainpipes, filling streets –_
   N _ever ever stopping._

Add the missing vowel to each syllable.

2. d i f / f _e_ r / _e_ n c e
3. r _e_ f / _e_ r / _e_ n c e
4. c _o_ n / f _e_ r / _e_ n c e

Complete these compound words.
Clue: all computer terms

5. net _work_
6. up _date_
7. down _load_
8. on _line_
9. tool _bar_
10. short _cut_

PART A Focus
1: acrostic form
2–4: unstressed vowels; spelling strategies
5–10: subject-specific compound words

B WORD WORK

1. Underline the odd one out.
   yield brief <u>weird</u> thief piece
2. Why is the odd one out unusual?
   Because it contains an 'ei' spelling and 'ie' is more common (except after 'c').

Add the same prefix to both words.

3. _pro_ ject   _pro_ duce
5. _ex_ ceed   _ex_ cept
4. _sus_ pect   _sus_ pense
6. _en_ close   _en_ joy

Write a definition of the word in **bold**.

7. Select the **channel** you want to view.
   channel: _station_
8. He was the first to swim the **Channel**.
   Channel: _the water between England and France_
9. It was a **joint** attempt.
   joint: _combined_
10. Your wrist **joint** allows you to move your hand.
    joint: _where two bones fit together_

PART B Focus
1–2: spelling patterns ei and ie
3–6: less-common prefixes
7–10: everyday subject-specific words

C SENTENCE WORK

These lovely creatures have lived here for centuries but sadly they are now endangered.

1. What is the writer's view of this situation? _That it is sad._
2. What is the writer's view of these creatures? _That they are lovely._
3. Which two words show the writer's opinion? _'sadly' and 'lovely'._

Continue the text with

4. a follow-up sentence: _We must do something to save them._
5. a follow-up question: _Is it the end for these beautiful animals?_
6. a follow-up imperative: _Help save them!_

7. What is the writer's purpose? Tick two.
   to instruct ___   to persuade ✓   to inform ✓   to entertain ___

Check the use of apostrophes.

8. Balloons~~'~~ were tied to the two donkey's tail's. *(corrections: donkeys' / tails)*
9. Hercules' carried the two sisters' shopping all the way to Marys' house.
10. The clock's finger's slowly ticked round as they waited for the chief's signal.

PART C Focus
1–3: identifying viewpoint
4–6: sentence types
7: writer's purpose
8–10: using apostrophes

X DEFINITIVE ANSWER   X SAMPLE ANSWER

Section 3　Test 11

A　WARM-UP

Write two sentences using these words.

doorway darkness

Use a different connective in each.

1. Megan peeped through the doorway, but all she could see was darkness.

2. As she peeped through the doorway, Megan waited for her eyes to adjust to the darkness.

Write the homophone.

3. **key**　quay
4. **waist**　waste
5. **him**　hymn
6. **serial**　cereal

Write two words using the root word.

7. **hyper**　hyperlink, hypermarket
8. **inter**　internet, interact
9. **mega**　megalith, megastar
10. **eco**　ecosystem, ecology

PART A Focus
1–2: compound sentences
3–6: homophones
7–10: common roots

B　WORD WORK

1. Add the missing syllable to each word.

   int / er / est　　gen / er / al
   sep / ar / ate　　av / er / age

2. What do you notice about the missing syllables?
   Each has an unstressed vowel.

3. separate is the odd one out because it uses 'ar', not 'er'.

PART B Focus
1–3: unstressed vowels
4–8: less common suffixes
9–10: root words

4. Add a suffix to make a verb.

   active　activate　　**mobile**　mobilise
   simple　simplify　　**dark**　darken

Use one of the verbs in each sentence.

5. The sky began to _darken_.
6. "_Activate_ the machine!" said Dr Brains.
7. We need to _simplify_ the wording.
8. The King began to _mobilise_ his forces.

Write three words linked in meaning and spelling to the word in **bold**.

9. **cycle**　recycle, bicycle, unicycle
10. **human**　inhuman, humanly, humane

C　SENTENCE WORK

Give two reasons why the writer might have changed this sentence as shown.

We know this is wrong.　Every right-thinking person knows this is utterly wrong.

1. To give the impression that everyone thinks this way.
2. So that the powerful adverb 'utterly' may be used to strengthen the point.

Rewrite this sentence so that it sounds more persuasive.

3. Every child should have a place to live.　Surely every child has the right to a safe home.

Complete the sentence using a simile.

4. He moved like an animal hunting its prey.
5. Kapil followed like a lost puppy.
6. She clucked like a fussy hen.
7. Azara behaves like a petulant child.

Write this text as direct speech, using a new line for each item.

The man wanted to speak to the Chief. I asked him to leave, but the man said it was urgent.

8. "I want to speak to the Chief," said the man.
9. "I'm sorry, that's not possible. You must leave," I replied.
10. "But I MUST speak to the Chief," insisted the man. "It's urgent."

PART C Focus
1–3: writing persuasively
4–7: similes
8–10: punctuating direct speech

Section 3 Test 12

A WARM-UP

Fruit is good for you.

Make this idea sound more appealing using

1 **alliteration:** Feast on five fun-filled fruity flavours!

2 **rhyme:** Plums and pears are good for you. You can try a smoothie too!

3 **a pun or word play:** Fruit – the pear-fect snack.

Add a three-letter word to complete the longer word.

4 v o l **can** o
5 c o m **put** e r
6 c o n **tin** u e
7 i n g **red** i e n t s

Add three of these suffixes to the root word to make three new words.

er en y ly ness

8 shake — shaker, shaky, shakily
9 wide — wider, widen, widely
10 glad — gladly, gladden, gladness

PART A Focus
1–3: word play
4–7: spelling strategies
8–10: root words; suffixes

B WORD WORK

Add the missing letters.

1 v **ei** n   **Clue:** carries blood round the body
2 r e c **ei** v e   **Clue:** to be given something
3 a n c **ie** n t   **Clue:** very old
4 f **ie** r c e   **Clue:** vicious

Add the suffix **ity** and write the new word.

5 secure — security
6 popular — popularity
7 human — humanity

8 What type of words have you made?
   nouns

PART B Focus
1–4: spelling patterns ei and ie
5–8: the suffix ity
9–10: subject-specific word meanings

Write two definitions of the word in **bold**.

9 **table**
   in maths: list of facts and numbers
   another meaning: item of furniture

10 **fast**
   in religious education (RE): a special time when you do not eat
   another meaning: quick

C SENTENCE WORK

Oliver sat up suddenly. The room was completely dark. What had woken him?

Write three ways in which the writer builds suspense.

1 Uses short sentences.
2 Uses a question.
3 Includes detail about the darkness.

Write the next sentence, further building the suspense.

4 In the distance a clock was ticking.

Rewrite the sentence with the ideas in a different order.

5 We need to raise more money to continue our valuable work.
   To continue our valuable work, we need to raise more money.

6 There will be no open spaces left if we continue to build more houses.
   If we continue to build more houses, there will be no open spaces left.

7 They waited for his return while the sun began to sink behind the rooftops.
   While the sun began to sink behind the rooftops, they waited for his return.

PART C Focus
1–4: narrative techniques
5–7: reordering clauses
8–10: sentence punctuation

Add commas, full stops and capital letters to make the meaning clear.

8 Overall, the film is stunning. From opening scene, to thrilling ending, you will be gripped.
9 He looked everywhere. He searched every box, every drawer, every hiding place.
10 We need to raise money. We need your help. Without it, more birds will die.

Remind the pupil to complete Section 3 of the Progress chart on page 46 of the workbook.

Schofield & Sims English Skills 4
Section 3 Writing task assessment sheet: Outraged

Name	Class/Set
Teacher's name	Date

Sentence structure and punctuation

	Always/often	Sometimes	Never
Uses varied sentence length (e.g., short to make a point; longer to explain)			
Uses different sentence types for persuasive effect (e.g., questions and imperatives)			
Uses adverbs and phrases to emphasise writer's view			
Uses a range of subordinating connectives			
Varies sentence structure and word order for effect			
Uses tense accurately and uses modal verbs to express shades of opinion (e.g., **might**, **could**, **will**)			
Demarcates sentences accurately (no comma splice)			
Uses commas to mark phrases and clauses			
Uses apostrophes correctly			
Uses other punctuation for effect (e.g., dash)			

Composition and effect

Shows clear sense of purpose to persuade the reader			
Ideas ordered as separate points or paragraphs			
Reasons and examples chosen for appeal to reader			
Uses connectives to link ideas and sentences			
Maintains Standard English			
Uses stylistic devices to engage reader (e.g., repetition, direct address)			
Uses emotive language to make text more persuasive			
Appropriate tone and style of address are maintained			

Spelling

Regular polysyllabic words correct			
Words with unstressed vowels correct			
Words with common letter strings correct			
Tricky medium-frequency words correct			
Prefixes and suffixes correctly spelt (e.g., **im**, **ir**, **al**)			
Applies rules for adding prefixes and suffixes			
Applies rules for forming plurals			
Applies rules for adding verb endings			
Consonant spelling patterns correctly applied (e.g., **ie**, **ei**)			
Common homophones correct			

*From: **English Skills 4 Answers** by Carol Matchett (ISBN 978 07217 1184 3). Copyright © Schofield & Sims Ltd, 2011. Published by Schofield & Sims Ltd, Dogley Mill, Fenay Bridge, Huddersfield HD8 0NQ, UK (www.schofieldandsims.co.uk).* **This page may be photocopied for use within your school or institution only.**

Schofield & Sims English Skills 4

Section 3 Completed proofreading task: The genie of the bedside lamp

Name	Class/Set
Teacher's name	Date

Scene 1
Seen 2: in the bedroom, which is a real mess.

Emily (in astonishment): Look at this mess! What happened? The carpet's ruined and Dad's prize CD collection is damaged. What's he going to say?

Ben (snappily): He's not going to say anything because it'll be tidy before he gets back.

Emily (in disbelief): Are you insane? That's impossible. You're definitely in trouble this time.

Ben (sighing): I'm probably going to regret this, but watch…

Ben picks up the bedside lamp and gives it a rub. There is a deafening roar. Emily lets out a shriek as a genie appears, floating by the ceiling.

Emily (trembling): What is that?

Ben (impatiently): A genie, of course!

Emily: But…but that's not possible, is it?

Please note: Some variation in punctuation is acceptable. For example, dashes and/or ellipses may be used to represent pauses in speech. Discuss the effect of using different methods of punctuation.

Section 3 tasks summary

Full list of the Schofield & Sims English Skills books

Workbooks

English Skills 1	978 07217 1175 1
English Skills 2	978 07217 1176 8
English Skills 3	978 07217 1177 5
English Skills 4	978 07217 1178 2
English Skills 5	978 07217 1179 9
English Skills 6	978 07217 1180 5

Answers

English Skills 1 Answers	978 07217 1181 2
English Skills 2 Answers	978 07217 1182 9
English Skills 3 Answers	978 07217 1183 6
English Skills 4 Answers	978 07217 1184 3
English Skills 5 Answers	978 07217 1185 0
English Skills 6 Answers	978 07217 1186 7

Teacher's Guide

The **Teacher's Guide** contains the **Workbook descriptors**, **Entry test** and many other useful items.

English Skills Teacher's Guide	978 07217 1187 4

Also available

Mental Arithmetic is similar in format to **English Skills**, providing intensive maths practice.